THE CLOWN PRINCE OF BASEBALL

The Clown Prince
of Baseball

by MAX PATKIN
and STAN HOCHMAN

WRS
PUBLISHING

A Division of WRS Group, Inc.
Waco, Texas

First published in the United States of America in 1993 by WRS Publishing,
A Division of WRS Group, Inc., 701 N. New Road, Waco, Texas 76710
Book design by Kenneth Turbeville
Jacket design by Joe James

10 9 8 7 6 5 4 3 2 1

Library of Congress Cataloging-in-Publication Data

Patkin, Max.
    The clown prince of baseball / by Max Patkin and Stan Hochman.
        p.   cm.
    ISBN 1-56796-036-7
    1. Patkin, Max. 2. Baseball coaches--United States--Biography.
    3. Clowns--United States--Biography.   I. Title.
GV865.P38A3 1994
796.357'092--dc20
    [B]   93-43574
                                                            CIP

Dedications

To Samuel and Rebecca Patkin, my parents,
who gave me the everlasting gift, teaching me to show
kindness and consideration to everyone.

—*Max Patkin*

To my wife, Gloria, for her love, which makes me the
luckiest man in America.

—*Stan Hochman*

Table of Contents

Foreword
by Joe Garagiola

I have seen Max Patkin perform in a dozen dusty ballparks across America, but my most vivid memory of Max doesn't involve that baggy old uniform he wears or the double-jointed signs he pretends to flash from the first base coaching box. Rather, it was an impromptu performance by Max on the veranda of the Otesaga Hotel in Cooperstown, a pop-up from baseball's Hall of Fame.

I was there with my family in 1991, and we were out there, on the patio, when Max went into his bobble-headed, elbows out, high-stepping strut—like a flamingo on hot coals.

My grandchildren couldn't believe what they were seeing. He had them in the palm of his hand. I looked around, and I saw older people watching and laughing too. At that moment I said, "That's why Max Patkin is so great."

You see, he doesn't appeal to just one particular group. He cuts across the whole spectrum, from toddlers to senior citizens. Almost everyone in baseball can remember the first time they saw Max, double-jointed, loose as a goose, his arms flapping, coaching first or third, lugging 20 bats to the plate for his one time at bat, sliding headfirst into third, the whole warm and wonderful act.

The first time I saw Max, he wasn't wearing that goofy uniform with the question mark on his back, and he wasn't using those red handkerchiefs to send signs by semaphore. He was dancing.

It was Philadelphia, probably at the Click, a spot some of the Cardinals visited to cool down after a ballgame at

Connie Mack Stadium. Max was on the dance floor dancing with a chorus girl, and quickly the floor cleared. It was the same reaction you'd see around a batting cage when Stan Musial hit, or Ted Williams. Guys cleared out, formed a semi-circle, watched the show. That's the way it was with Max, dancing.

I've always felt that one of the funniest parts of Max's act is when he dances to that Bill Haley number, "Rock Around the Clock." He's out there dancing, and yet it's the best parody of a third base coach you will ever see. If I were still doing the pre-game baseball show on the network I'd use a split screen—Max on one side, Larry Bowa or Jimy Williams on the other giving signs, the music in the background.

Max has a wider range than Al Schacht, who started the idea. And when Max hangs his cap up, it will be the end of the line. Max sticks to baseball. The mascots, the costumed guys, aren't tuned in to the rhythms of the game the way that Max is. The Chicken, he needs cue cards. The Phillie Phanatic, he's the best of the current bunch, a lively, acrobatic young guy, but even he strays from the game much of the time, hugging the women, bugging the vendors.

People are always amazed that Max has survived as long as he has, because he does his act while the game is going on around him. But the proof of a good performer is whether they ask you back. And Max has been going back to the same minor league ballparks year after year after year. A zealot is a zealot is a zealot, just as a purist is a purist is a purist. The guy who is unhappy with Max being out there is the kind of guy who gripes about the candles in church—saying the smoke bothers him.

Baseball is entertainment. It's a game.

But it's hard work for Max. Few people realize just how physical it gets. We found out, when we followed Max to Tidewater to film a segment for the "Today" show. It was raining, but Max went out there, doing a solo, playing to the crowd, going all out. And then he grabbed the bag of baseballs and started tossing them to the crowd. Somebody grabbed one of the balls and fired it back at him. Hit him in the head. He went down like a rock. We thought he'd had a heart attack. They rushed him to the hospital. Later that night, he came trudging into the empty hotel lobby, looking like a sack of laundry after a hard wash—just wrung-out. He was carrying a duffel bag, looking like Willy Loman, in *Death of a Salesman*.

What a tough way to make a living. I'm sure the money is important, but I get the feeling that Max thrives more on the crowd's reaction. He needs that laughter to keep going.

He is also a genuinely good guy. Which is amazing, considering how much sadness he's had in his life. I can remember that dinner for Tommy Lasorda in Norristown when Max showed up with a turban of bandages on his head. Max is funny looking on his own, with that one front tooth that makes him look like Kukla, from Kukla, Fran and Olly, but the turban was a topper. And he tells me that the bandages are hiding the dents in his head because his wife hit him with a ballpeen hammer. I introduce him to the crowd, tell them what Max told me, and the crowd laughs, because the story seems like a gag. Some gag. There's a lot of Pagliacci in Max.

He's had his share of tragedy, but you'd never know it. Even when he talks about it, at the end, he tries to give you a laugh.

My grandson Ross is four now. But he can still remember Max, and he will still try to imitate that bird-like walk, and he will still laugh at the memory of it.

Preface

by Ron Shelton
Writer and Director of *Bull Durham*

"If every fool wore a crown,
we should all be kings."
—*Erasmus, "In Praise of Folly"*

I walked away from baseball for twenty years, unable to watch a game or read the sports page. A lifetime dream of being a major league ballplayer died in the minor leagues—in some dusty town in a ballpark with bad lights, cramped dugouts, and dripping shower heads. I had to get on with my life, as they say, and so I went back to school, worked wherever I could find it, and filled out job applications by the thousands. Somewhere, sometime later, I started calling myself a writer because I had to call myself something. The problem was, of course, that writers needed something to write about, and what I really knew about was the minor leagues. But I thought I still couldn't face baseball.

I drove to North Carolina to see if I could slip quietly into one of those dusty old ballparks and watch a game from a distance, to see if baseball still had a stranglehold on me, to see if I could face the past, the failure—to see, really, if I'd grown up. Loaded with invented sorrow, I slipped past the bleachers to see the field, and suddenly Bill Haley and the Comets was blaring on the worst and loudest speakers in the world, "one o'clock, two o'clock, three o'clock rock..."

And there he was, Max Patkin, preening at home plate, spitting water, strutting down the foul line, dancing, writhing—the same routine I had seen dozens of times in my minor league travels twenty years earlier. I started laughing, and in many ways I've been laughing ever since. I was a kid at the ballpark again, and I wondered why I'd stayed away so long. The problem was not that I hadn't grown up, but that I *had* grown up—too much and too soon.

Therein lies the power of the clown—he makes us laugh to remind us where we hurt, and somehow the pain is lessened. Since all humor is rooted in pain, Max's and our own, the laughter he evokes in concert with the heroics of the athletes around him acts as both mockery and a tribute to their achievements. When you leave the ballpark, part of you wants to identify with the next Jose Canseco, knocking homers into the night sky of El Paso with a body chiselled by Michelangelo. But the rest of you is still smiling at the clown, because he is closer to us than any Hall of Famer. He is us.

I had many beers with Max in the minors, because even then the clown fascinated me. As the world was turning to video games and mass marketed, corporate-designed mascots that all looked the same and behaved the same, Patkin stuck with his version of a clown—one that did not need a furry costume. It was not a chicken or a swollen headed day-glo geek or a whatsit. It was a man.

With a fabulous face and the limber body of a too-tall dancer, this clown was human. There was nothing god-like or anthropomorphic about this clown. He was, well, sort of regular—like a baseball player. And while stadiums got domed and grass turned plastic and baseball went all to hell, Patkin continued showing up in minor league parks throughout the country, building what is surely the longest career of one-night stands in show business history. Big crowds, little crowds, no crowds—Max was the ultimate vaudevillian, never missing a show for over forty years.

Patkin coaches first base, then third base, continually interrupting the game, spitting water on the players, and presumably sometimes waving a runner in from second or telling him to hold at third—how many sports would allow a clown to do this? Only baseball. The game, affected and interpreted by the clown, continues on its way.

After a few days in the Carolina League, I returned home to California and announced to my friends that I was going to make a movie about baseball, the *real* game, I said, the way it used to be and is supposed to be still. Great, they said, what's it about? I don't know, I said, but I know one thing. It starts with Max Patkin.

Acknowledgments

The Max Patkin that baseball fans see on a ballfield, rowdy, raucous, irreverent, is not the same Max Patkin away from the roar of the crowd. In working on this book, I discovered a humble, sensitive, gregarious man, with a legion of friends in baseball.

I owe thanks to Max for his colorful story telling, to his brother Eddie for filling in some gaps in Max's memory, and I appreciated the help I got from Max's daughter, Joy, in understanding what Max's marriage was like.

Lou Reda, who has known Max since their Navy days together in the South Pacific, was a great help in keeping both of us focused.

Joe James and Kenneth Turbeville for their inspired artwork.

Mark Patz did a meticulous job of editing the manuscript.

Joe Garagiola, president of BAT (Baseball Assistance Team), took time out during the World Series to do his foreword.

Ron Shelton, writer/director of *Bull Durham*, also kindly provided an eloquent, additional foreword.

Lorenzo Biggs of the *Philadelphia Daily News* double-checked name, dates, and places.

And My wife Gloria deserves a special thanks for allowing me to use major portions of our summer vacation to work on the book.

It was a fun experience and I hope it reads that way.

—*Stan Hochman*

Introduction
by Stan Hochman

He had been in Bend, Oregon, the day before. Daybreak flight, Bend to Frisco, Frisco to Washington, Washington to Philadelphia. And now, on a gloomy Monday afternoon, the sky the color of ashes, he was sprawled in the back seat, heading for Wilmington, Delaware.

How tired was Max Patkin? Tired enough to let his brother, Eddie, drive from their apartment in King of Prussia, to Wilmington.

How tired was Max Patkin? Tired enough not to squawk when Eddie missed the I-95 exit for Legends Field, where the Blue Rocks play.

Patkin was 73. That night he looked 83, sounded 93. He was bone weary, and you could almost hear him creak when he walked. His eyes were bloodshot from fatigue, the lids at half-mast.

A sudden thundershower had drenched the ballpark. The infield, left uncovered, was now a swamp. Patkin had been rained out on his scheduled date and this was a make-up appearance.

Patkin talked wearily to the Wilmington players about their part in his performance. He talked briefly to the Kinston first baseman about the bit where he shadows his every move. He visited with the umpires, rehashed his trademark finish. And then he trudged into the Wilmington clubhouse. The grounds crew managed to get the infield playable. Ushers and usherettes helped roll the tarp. The crowd sat patiently through a half-hour delay.

Patkin sprawled on the clubhouse sofa, blinking himself awake.

Eddie remained in the car, in the paved parking lot. He wasn't bored, he explained, he was simply sad. "I hate to see an old man do a youngster's work," he explained.

In the third inning, Max Patkin pranced out of the dugout, dressed in a raggedy, mismatched uniform with a huge question-mark on his back. The dirt-stained red-and-blue Montreal cap perched jauntily on his head. The Wilmington pitcher had a no-hitter, a perfect game through three innings, when Max strutted out there, to coach first base. Not the best of circumstances for comedy.

The game was scurrying along, hitters swinging at almost every pitch. Not the best of circumstances for sight gags and pratfalls, corny props and cornier dialogue with the box seat customers.

He scrunched his rubbery face and said to some giggling kids, "Behave, or you're gonna grow up and look like me." He opened his mouth wide, revealing that one crooked tooth. "I've got a toothbrush with one bristle," he yelped.

A heckler stomped down the steps towards the field, screaming something about getting that foolishness off the field. Max glared at him, and yelled, "Get a job." The fan retreated, embarrassed.

Behind home plate, a clatter of fans began to argue about Patkin's age. A man who promotes appearances by former athletes at autograph shows was sure that Patkin had worked for the Dodgers at one time. He was thinking about Emmit Kelly, the famous circus clown, who had been briefly employed by the Dodgers, dressed in raggedy clothes after cartoonist Willard Mullin had depicted the Dodgers as "Dem Bums."

Patkin flashed signals to the hitters, whipped out two red hankies to use semaphore, bent from the waist, his head at ankle level, pretending to steal signs from the catcher.

The Kinston pitcher fell behind one Wilmington hitter, 2-and-0. "You've got two balls," Patkin screeched. "One more and you can join the circus." Patkin says his act is 90 percent clean and 15 percent raunchy. He has trouble with arithmetic.

For me, the highlight of the act was "Old Faithful." He sipped from a battered soda can, and then he tilted his head back, patted his stomach, his chest, like a cop frisking a suspect, and out comes this fine spray from his mouth.

Once, twice, three times. He'd pause to encourage the hitter with frantic pantomime. He'd gesture to the crowd. And then, he'd resume the spray. He did it 31 times, from a single gulping of water. I watched him undress later; there were no hidden contraptions, no secret hiding places.

At the bottom of the fifth, after Max had been out there for three innings, Wilmington led, 2–0, and the pitcher, Robert Toth, still had his perfect game, 15 up, 15 down. Now, he had to throw three pitches to Patkin, who was lugging nine bats towards home plate, staggering under the weight.

He dumped eight of them, falling to his knees, but some of them twisted into a pile of lumber that rattled off his back. Still on his knees, he crawled between the catcher's legs.

Toth was thinking no-hitter, and now he had to pitch to this weary old clown. First pitch was in the dirt. Second pitch was low and inside. Patkin thumped the catcher on his shoulder, who followed the script, and toppled on his backside.

Patkin hit the third, half-hearted pitch towards the second baseman. Patkin headed for third base, slowly, ever so slowly, like a man lugging a piano. The third baseman took the throw. And now, as planned, he gazed skyward when Patkin approached pointing to the moon. Patkin dove into third base, the ground still soggy from the afternoon shower.

The umpire gestured "out" and Patkin scrambled to his feet to argue. He threw that dirt-stained red and blue cap to the grass. The umpire waved his right arm towards the dugout, towards the clubhouse, towards the comfort of the showers.

Patkin walked slowly towards the dugout, the crowd on its feet, cheering and laughing. A standing ovation from 5,300 and suddenly it was all worthwhile.

Patkin paused, near home plate, and blew a kiss to the crowd. And then he was gone.

He undressed slowly. He sat there, on a clubhouse stool, dirty and sweaty and weary. He offered the clubhouse boy five dollars to scrape the mud off his cleats. He showered, dressed, waited patiently for someone to retrieve his tape of "Rock Around the Clock," then stoically accepted his check from the general manager.

He beamed when the young man said that Max had gotten the first standing ovation in the team's history for a non-playing performer. He signed autographs for fans leaving early for 15 minutes (the no-hitter had vanished in the sixth, the shutout in the seventh). And then Patkin eased into the back seat of the car. It was late. He had altered his usual routine of having his uniform washed at the ballpark.

"They've got rules," Eddie said, fretting about the chore of washing the uniform back at the apartment complex. "Can't use the washer after nine o' clock. Hey, what the hell, one time, I've gotta do it. He leaves for South Dakota tomorrow."

"What about the guitar player?" Patkin sighed from the back seat. "He plays all hours of the night. Chords. Just chords."

Another night, another show, another flight ahead. At 73, he had done a youngster's work. The laughter, the cheers, the standing ovation muffled the pain in those 73-year-old knees one more time.

Chapter 1

EJECTED, REJECTED, DEJECTED

I've been thrown out of more ballparks than yesterday's trash.

I've been chased in Chihuahua, thumbed in Tucson, and ejected in Eau Claire. From Portland, Maine to Portland, Oregon, if there's a minor league ballpark, I've played it, and I've sprayed it—maybe you saw me in the movie *Bull Durham* doing my "Old Faithful" routine, sipping from a soda can, cocking my handsome head back, and spritzing a fine, geyser-like spray 10, 15, 20 times.

I'm Max Patkin, the Clown Prince of Baseball, which, like a lot of other royal titles, will get me on a subway if I've also got $1.25. I live in King of Prussia now, just outside of Philadelphia, where I was born (a prince living in King of Prussia, Camelot, it ain't). I am 73 years old, with a battered body and a few crooked teeth left in my mouth. Bill Veeck, who gave me my start, once said that I looked like I was assembled by somebody who had trouble reading the instructions. I've been on the road forever. This is my sixth decade in baseball. I've never stopped to count how many times I've played Boise or Butte or Buffalo, but I know I've done my act maybe 4,100 times.

What was Lou Gehrig's record for consecutive games played, 2,130? Well, for 50 years, I never, ever missed a game because of illness or injury, so I guess that made me the "Iron Man" of baseball clowns.

Rain, sleet, snow, gloom of night didn't stop me. Sadness, sorrow, and a shrewish wife who tried to bust my head open with a hammer didn't stop me. Never, ever missed a game even though I'd busted every finger on my left hand at one time or another, cracked ribs, pulled hamstrings, and needed stitches to sew up a gash on my forehead because a home-team trainer missed his cue in Elmira.

I'm patched together with surgical thread and friction tape now. So, I've eliminated some of the really crazy stuff I used to do, like when I kick my shoe off and then act surprised to see it plop there, in foul territory. I'd strut over there, pick it up, show it to the crowd, ask if it belonged to anyone. And then, I'd sniff it. And I'd fall over, pretending to faint from the odor. Straight backwards, I finally ruptured a disk and ended up in surgery.

Anyway, I used to sprawl there, limp and lifeless, which was the cue for the home-team trainer to come bustling out with a bucket of water. He was supposed to toss the water on me, and I'd wake up and go back to clowning in the first base coaching box. Well, in Elmira that night, I kicked off the shoe, sniffed it, fainted, and sprawled.

I'm down eight, nine, ten seconds and nothing happens. That's too long. Comedy is timing, and I'm out there, limp, too long. So, I sit up, to see what's going on. And there's Freckles Fertchik, the trainer, standing there, swinging a galvanized bucket full of ice water.

Wham, he hits me, right between the eyes with the bucket.

The blood started spurting out. He runs, gets me a towel. I needed 10 stitches after the game, but I finished my act.

Branch Rickey was there that night, because the Dodgers' general manager, the man who broke the color barrier with Jackie Robinson, was looking at a pitcher he considered promoting to the major league club. Afterwards, Rickey said to me, "Max, that was hysterical. Why don't you keep it in the act?"

Sure, that was easy for him to say.

If nothing else, I am hard-headed. A steel bucket, right between the eyes, did not keep me from my next date. My streak continued.

It ended in the summer of '93, at a big league ballpark, Fenway Park. Not with a whimper, but with a bang. I somehow blew the bottom step coming out of the Boston clubhouse. Went splat, severely spraining my left ankle. Had to cancel a date in New Britain the next day. Shattered the streak, *50 years* without ever missing a game.

Hey, it's a corny act. I know it, you know it, the players know it. But the fans still like it. I wouldn't be out there, summer night after summer night, getting filthy, getting sweaty, getting weary, if I wasn't also getting laughs.

I do my act during the game, on the field. That sets me apart from all those costumed mascots you see in the big league ballparks, guys waddling around in the stands dressed like chickens or pirates or cartoon characters.

That's *me* they're laughing at, Max Patkin, big nose, long neck, loose as a goose Max Patkin. And, at 73, I can still spread-eagle my legs and bend from the waist until my big nose is touching the ground, pretending to steal the signs from the visiting team's catcher.

Most people think it's funny. Pitchers are not like most people. Lee Smith, the ace reliever for the Cardinals, was pitching for Midland. I'm in Tulsa, a Texas League game, coaching first, and I bend down, peer in at the catcher, pretend I've swiped the sign.

I walk in four or five steps towards the hitter and I holler, "Fast ball, be ready."

Well, Smith throws a fast ball and the guy hits it out of the park. The inning ends, Smith crosses my path heading for his dugout and he snarls, "You do that again and I'm gonna knock you on your butt."

It wasn't so much the language, it was the way he looked at me, made my hair stand up.

That wasn't the first time somebody was unhappy with my act. It won't be the last time. I know the purists hate me clowning around out there while a game is going on. They act like baseball is some kind of religious experience, and that I'm out there scrawling a mustache on the Mona Lisa.

Hey, I know my place. I try not to interfere with the flow of the game.

I just want to entertain the fans, and if I do three innings out there, I'm tossed by the umpire before the game gets down to crunch time.

There are times when the fans can't get enough of me. Like the time in Duluth, in the old Northern League.

I'm coaching third base. It's a Class D league and most of the kids had never seen me before, so they didn't know exactly what I was gonna do next.

I call "time" and I gesture for the hitter to come out of the batter's box. I walk down the third base line, meet him maybe halfway. I act like I'm gonna tell him something important, like I want to whisper in his ear. And then, I plant a big kiss on his cheek. The guy shuffles back to the plate, blushing, and sure enough, he gets a base hit.

Now, the crowd is yelling for me to kiss the next guy. I call "time," walk down, kiss the guy. Bingo, he gets a base hit.

Now the crowd is really into it. They're screaming, "Kiss the next guy." So I do it. And, bango, he gets a base hit. The third batter motions for me to come down and kiss him. I do it. Seven straight base hits—a true story. The visiting team changes pitchers, I go over to the stands, I'm kissing fans, the crowd is going nuts. I yell that the week before, I kissed a hitter on the mouth and he followed me home.

Finally, the eighth guy pops out. I get a great ovation.

These days I'll kibitz with the fans, but I won't leave the field and go into the stands. I'll ask, "Are there any lonely women up there in the audience?"

And somebody always yells, "I'll never get *that* lonely."

And sometimes, if they're changing pitchers I'll tell the crowd, "Here I am, back in Calgary (or Bowie or Terre Haute or...). I was here 35 years ago, you know. I was visiting one of my old girlfriends here. Took me two hours to find the nursing home she's in."

Or I'll tell the kids, "If you don't behave, you're gonna grow up to look like me." Quiets them down every time.

I stopped going into the stands after a game in

Nashville, about six or seven years ago. I'm mingling with the fans, behind home plate, and I see two women sitting there. I grab a pocketbook from one of them and she's clutching it, trying to snatch it back. We're wrestling for it and, bang, a gun falls out. Hits the concrete. If it had gone off, it would have put a bullet through my belly. The general manager was really upset. He told me he didn't ever want me going into the stands again. It turned out they were women police officers, off duty.

I guess I didn't totally learn my lesson, because for a while I was still climbing into the stands during a lull in the action, a pitching change, whatever. I'd pretend I was going to lift something out of a pocketbook or that I was going to kiss some woman. Well, there was this kid, sitting in his mother's lap, and I went to smooch her and, wham, the kid punched me in the face, bloodied my nose. I guess he didn't want somebody this handsome kissing his mother.

The act hasn't changed that much in 45 years. I made the whole thing up. I've been subtracting stuff more than adding down through the years.

I took out the football thing, where I'd prop a glove up on the coaching line and I'd take a run towards it, full speed, and act like I was going to kick a field goal. I'd miss, fall on my butt. And I took out the old bathing suit bit, where I'd strip off my uniform and be wearing an old-fashioned striped bathing suit. The outfit in Portland doesn't make them anymore. And besides, I weighed 145 then—looked like a lollipop stick with a nose. I've added a few pounds down through the years, so the thing wouldn't look that funny.

I put "Old Faithful" in about 40 years ago. I'd come out of the dugout with two Coca-Cola bottles and I'd spray the ballplayers, telling them I wanted them to hustle. I'd spray and then I'd flip the bottles towards the dugout. Nobody wants a bunch of broken glass in the dugouts, so I gave up the bottles and switched to cans. Ordinarily, I'll spray 15, 20 times out of one gulp. The guys in the bullpen usually count for me. My all-time record is 40.

What's changed is some of the stuff leading up to my act. I've been delivered to the first base coach's box by helicopter in Little Rock. I've been driven in the Oscar Mayer hot dog van in Reading. I've even been taken out there in a hot rod dragster at a college game, Southwest Louisiana against Lamar.

Which reminds me of the first time I ever ran into Sparky Anderson, who manages Detroit now. He was managing Rock Hill, a little, crumby ballpark. And next door, they've got a midget auto racetrack. The game starts and all you can hear is r-r-r-r-r, r-r-r-r-r, the cars racing around the track. Saturday night, and they had five times more people at the racetrack than in the ballpark, and you couldn't hear a thing.

One of the toughest shows I ever did.

Maybe not the toughest, because that had to be in Great Falls, Montana. Drew four people—it was 1969, the Sunday afternoon the astronauts landed on the moon. The general manager asked me if I would cancel, and I didn't want to blow the pay day, so I said I'd go on. He said he'd scatter some television sets around the ballpark, but only four people showed up, and two of them were the parents of the starting pitcher.

I did my whole act and afterwards the general manager said, "Max, I can't believe you worked that hard with nobody in the ballpark."

And I told him, "All those kids were rookies, they'd never seen me before. They were enjoying it."

The kids in rookie ball or Class A, they're great, unspoiled. They get to the majors, they change. The writers change them, blow too much smoke their way, their egos get bent out of shape.

That day in Great Falls, I ended my act the way I always end it. The public address announcer says that Max Patkin will now show the Wilmington Blue Rocks or the Toledo Mudhens something about hitting. I grab maybe eight or nine bats from the rack and stagger towards home plate. (I used to grab 20, until the night I toppled over and one of the bats cracked my rib.) I go to my knees, slither through the catcher's legs, and then take my stance.

The first pitch is supposed to be high and tight. I duck out of the way. Sure, I've been hit a few times. This is not my real face. The second pitch is down the middle, hard. I shove the catcher and he falls on his butt and gets up, pretending to be angry. The next pitch is one I can hit. I hit it, and then I run towards third base. They throw the ball to third, I stop just short of the bag, point to the sky, and the third baseman looks up. I dive head-first into the bag, stir up a cloud of dust, but the umpire always calls me out. I throw my cap, I bluster around, get in his face, arguing. And then he thumbs me, throws me out of the game.

It's a good bit, always gets a laugh, a nice way to finish.

Except for one time when Bruce Froemming was the plate umpire in Eugene, Oregon. I forget the guy working third base, but he let Froemming talk him into something.

I run to third, I slide in, on my stomach, he calls me out, I start to argue. Now, suddenly, the umpire sticks his hand in his pocket and pulls out a gun. He points it right at my face and he yells, "Max, I've taken enough of your garbage through the years," and he pulls the trigger. Bang!

And then he shoots again. Bang!

I should have known I was alright when I heard the second shot. But I was too startled, too stunned to react. I was scared witless. The ump sees me standing there, and finally he says, "Fall down, dummy."

I fall down, milk it a little, get up and walk off, still shaking inside my baggy pants. They say your life passes before your eyes at moments like that. I don't know about that. I've had too crazy a life, too funny, too sad, to blur past my eyes in an instant.

This way is better, writing a book.

I really wanted to be a big league pitcher. And I was still clinging to that dream when Joe DiMaggio turned my life around that day in Honolulu, when he hit a home run off me that is probably still bobbling around in the Pacific Ocean.

Chapter 2

JOLTED BY JOLTIN' JOE

I never dreamed about being a clown.

I never told some sixth grade teacher that my ambition in life was to be a comic, that my hero was Marcel Marceau or Joe E. Brown or Charlie Chaplin. In sixth grade, my only ambition was to avoid getting sent to the principal's office that day. When I graduated from high school, they should have given the diploma to my mother. She spent more time at the school than I did.

It wasn't like I went to the circus one day and I saw Emmit Kelly sweeping in that spotlight, in those baggy pants and that dirty homburg, and heard the laughter and decided that was the life for me...

I wanted to be a big league pitcher.

Could have been one. Had this terrific windup. Kicked high. Higher than Juan Marichal ever kicked. Higher than the Radio City Music Hall Rockettes ever kicked. I'd rock back and throw my left leg high in the air and the batter would stare at that and whoosh, I'd throw my fast ball right by him. They didn't have radar guns in those days but I know I threw 90, 92 MPH.

I didn't always know where the pitch was going, but it got there in a hurry.

I pitched in high school and at Brown Prep. And I pitched in the Wisconsin State League for two years. Led the league in wild pitches one year. But got my arm torn up trying to tag a guy out at the plate.

That was one of the reasons I enlisted in the Navy. My draft number came up early and I preferred the Navy to the Army, even though I got seasick in a rowboat. Thought the food would be better, thought living conditions would be better. Turned out to be a smart move.

I was stationed at Cape May, New Jersey, for a while—minesweeper duty. They were going to send me to sonar school in New London when I heard about a program at Bainbridge that trained physical instructors. I got accepted there. Bayonet drill, swim drill—a tough course, with a 4:30 wakeup call. I managed to get through the six weeks and they sent me to Great Lakes. I'm company commanding officer, supervising 120 men.

At Great Lakes Dr. Bear operated on my arm, took six centimeters of bone chips out, just over the ulnar nerve, told me I'd need three months to recover. I can't remember his first name. We probably called him "Grizzly." When the time was up, I still had some pop on my fast ball, though.

They shipped me out for the Pacific, heading for New Caledonia. I'm on a flat-top, the Lexington, and we stop in Honolulu. Out of the blue, they make this announcement, if anybody has any professional baseball experience, report to a certain officer. I go, tell him I played in the Wisconsin State League, for Green Bay. They take me off the ship and assign me to the base.

Suddenly, I'm on a team with Peewee Reese, Hugh Casey, guys like that, and I'm pitching for AIEA Hospital.

They had a six-team league, Army, Navy, Marine, Air Force teams. I'm assigned to the AIEA Barracks after word got around about my showmanship. I'm in charge of guys like Mickey Vernon, Gene Woodling, Pinky May.

Vernon managed for about 20 years in the minors and every time I'd come into his ballpark after the war to do my act, he'd yank me aside, and say, "Please, Max, don't tell my ballplayers you were my commanding officer, they'll lose respect for me."

Bill Dickey, the great Yankee catcher, was my commanding officer. We're playing the 7th Air Force, tied for first place. They must have had a crowd of 10,000 servicemen there.

I didn't start that ballgame that day. Lefty Holland did, and they got six or seven runs off him before he got anybody out. So they call on me. They've got Ferris Fain at first, Joe Gordon at second, Gerry Priddy playing short, Bob Dillinger at third. The outfield is Walter Judnich, Mike McCormick, and Joe DiMaggio, with Charlie Silvera catching and Red Ruffing pitching.

I'm getting them out. Strike DiMaggio out the first time I face him. Whiff four or five other guys. Second time up, DiMaggio nearly kills our shortstop, Eddie Pelligrini with a line drive single.

Now, it's the sixth or seventh inning and I start to do my stuff, stretch my neck, whirl my arms, bend over from the waist until my chin is almost on the ground. DiMaggio comes up and I turn around and gesture to my outfielders, that they can move in. I don't know why I did that. Maybe it was because I'd struck him out the first time.

I'd gotten him on a fast ball, so now I'm gonna throw him a changeup.

I throw it, he hits it over the centerfield fence, maybe 500 feet. We were using those "97" baseballs, which took off like rockets, and the air was light. He rounds first base and I think, what the heck, I'll give these guys a laugh, I'll follow him around the bases. DiMaggio had this unique stride, and I fall in behind him, imitating that stride all the way around the bases.

The fans are hysterical. His whole team comes swarming out of the dugout towards home plate. And now, they ignore Joe, and they shake my hand, walk me back to the mound, patting me on the back.

The score is 9–0 and they're patting me on the back and the crowd is going nuts, including the brass, the admirals and generals. The whole thing got written up in "Stars and Stripes" and generals started calling our barracks to ask when the goofy guy was gonna pitch again.

They started calling me "Elmer" after the character that Joe E. Brown played, Elmer the Great. And, after they found out I loved to dance, some guys called me Ray Bolger.

I'd never had confidence I could make people laugh. In the minors, if you do crazy stuff, you're a clown. In the big leagues, they say you have color.

I still thought I could be a big league pitcher, but now, people were laughing and I was getting writeups in the *Honolulu Advertiser* and guys were asking, where's Elmer?

One game, fifth inning, an ambulance, siren wailing, comes onto the field. Medics come out with a stretcher. I'm on it, wrapped up, head to toe, like a mummy. The Corpsmen had done it.

They set me down, unwrapped me, and I went out to coach first.

I met Bobby Riggs while I was stationed at Honolulu. He was a little hustler, teaching the nurses how to play tennis in return for certain favors. He'd get guys on the basketball court, win a lot of money shooting hoops. Bought a car with his winnings. Buddy Blattner was there too, second baseman, good ballplayer, wound up being Dizzy Dean's broadcast partner years later. He was also a very good ping-pong player. He'd put on exhibitions with Riggs, who was the national champion in tennis at the time.

I thought I was a decent ping-pong player too and one day I challenged Riggs. He had to give me points. I told him, "Give me 13, and I think I can beat you."

He said, "For how much?"

We started out playing for $25, which was a lot of money in those days. Before you know it, I beat him three or four games. Now, we boost the bet to $100 a game.

We play six games, I've got him stuck for a couple of hundred dollars.

The next day, the word has gotten around, and we've got a huge crowd. Now, he's wearing his white tennis outfit, sneakers, he's brought his own net. We're going to play for $100 a game and I beat him two or three games in a row. He wants to lower the spot, but I tell him we'd agreed I'd never take less than 12 points. We keep playing, I keep beating him. I've got him stuck for about $1,500 when he gets shipped out.

He gave me a couple of hundred before he left, but he still owed me $1,300. I've see him through the years, I'd try to collect. He'd say, "Max, it's a war debt." And then he'd promise to take me to dinner. How many dinners can I eat for $1,300? I guess it was alright. I got bragging rights forever, saying I beat Bobby Riggs.

When Riggs played Billie Jean King in that tennis match at the Astrodome in Houston, I rooted for Riggs, for old time's sake. He was way past his prime, but he was still a great showman. Nobody got hurt, women's tennis got a boost, Riggs got his name and face on national television, and a lot of people made money.

When I wasn't pitching, hustling ping-pong bets, or free throw shooting bets in Honolulu, I'd be off dancing, usually at the Royal Hawaiian. Eddie Peabody was in charge there. It was R-and-R for the submarine personnel.

I'd do all this eccentric, goofy dancing, loose-jointed stuff, the kind of stuff Ray Bolger did in those days. This got me in some hot water once when I was invited to perform at the University of Hawaii. The young lady who lined up the performance had told the school president that Ray Bolger was coming.

I get there, and there's this big sign out front, "Welcome Ray Bolger." They've got 700 people in the gym, so I grab the president and say, "Can I talk to you for a second?"

I told him I wasn't Ray Bolger, that I was Max Patkin. He was flustered, but then he said to tell them I use Ray Bolger as a nickname. So that's what I did and I put on the exhibition.

They had dances two or three times a week at Waikiki, a place called Mallihia, with big orchestras. I remember that a woman named Mabel was in charge. She'd blow a whistle and the servicemen would come running out onto the dance floor to cut in, because the men outnumbered the women 5-to-1.

She wouldn't let anyone cut in on me.

I did exhibition dancing at the USO, and I did exhibitions for the Army, Navy, and Marine bases there.

Lou Reda, who became my buddy, was a band singer.

He'd sing with Ray Anthony's band at the Royal Hawaiian. Then, we'd hitchhike back to the base. Lou would stay in the background, and I'd plant my feet on the curb and lean out from the waist. I'd stretch my arms out over the road. That didn't give the cars much room to pass. They had to stop.

Mostly, they stopped because they couldn't believe what they saw. This sailor, bent in half, with long arms, and a head propped on a skinny neck—we never failed to get a ride back.

We were almost always out after curfew, but we had passes personally signed by Admiral Nimitz. (I wish I had saved that pass. It would probably be worth some money today. I wish I had saved one-tenth of the memorabilia I accumulated down through the years; I could retire tomorrow.)

Years later, Lou came to see me perform in Allentown. He was representing Johnny Desmond, the great band singer—Lou was into that, representing entertainers. He said he'd like to be my agent, but I had a guy who was booking me at the time. And I wanted to stay loyal to him, even though Lou seemed sharper, and talked about making me famous.

Now, 40 years later, Lou is my agent on this book. One thing you can say about him, he's patient.

To get a discharge, you needed a certain number of points, based on length of service, combat zones, that sort of stuff. I got a letter from the Cleveland Indians saying they were going to sign me when I got out of the service. If you had a job waiting, you had a better shot of getting out.

Before I shipped back to the States, I spent $100 for a chief's coat—a zoot-suit version of a chief's coat—plus pegged pants. Got it made at Battleship Abe's, a tailor shop in Honolulu. I get off the ship in San Diego and put it on for the first time. My buddies look at me and say, "Are you crazy?"

I'm in San Diego for maybe 10 minutes, the Shore

Patrol grabs me. Improper uniform. They send me back to the ship.

When I finally get home, I'm still in uniform. My friend Lou Reda and I go to the Roseland in New York. I'm dancing, and pretty soon a crowd gathers, and the owner invites me back to do an exhibition on the 25th anniversary of the Roseland. They've got Ray Bolger, Sally and Tony DeMarco performing. They let me do some dancing. I remember Bolger telling me, I had to do a little more if I wanted to be in show biz.

We went to Leon and Eddie's. Someone had told Eddie Davis that Lou could sing. He got up, sang a few songs. And then they offered me a job as a dancer. I felt bad. I turned it down.

Cleveland had given me a Wilkes-Barre contract. That was Class A baseball. Got a bonus, got a deal for $350 a month, which seemed like a lot of money.

This was 1946. I go to spring training. I'm not a kid. I'm 26. I look around, see a lot of good, young pitchers. I thought I had enough stuff to make hitters cringe. How did I know I'd last for six decades in baseball, making people laugh?

Chapter 3

ONLY MOTHER LOVED THIS FACE

How old am I?

Old enough, so that our first family car was a model-T Ford. My father drove it out of the showroom and slammed into a parked car on the street. Bam, it went right back into the shop.

I can remember being fascinated by the horses on the street. Horses pulled milk wagons in those days. A horse pulled the pickle-ah. That's what we called the cart that carried barrels of sour pickles. Fruit and vegetable guys came clomping down the street with horse-drawn carts.

My father repaired and resold checkwriters. In those days, businesses used mechanical checkwriters for their payrolls. He'd buy beat-up machinery and then bring it home, repair it, and sell it. But things were tough, especially in the Depression years. If he wanted $30 for a repaired checkwriter and the guy only had $10 in cash, he'd take merchandise for the other $20.

Which is why we had the best toys in the neighborhood. For as long as they lasted. I don't know how many pairs of roller-skates I went through. I'd get a pair, my father would come off the road, a neighbor would tell him how I'd bounced off a car in the street, bingo, he'd take away the skates.

He was proud of me once I started pitching. Once, I was pitching for Brown Prep, against Admiral Farragut. We were driving to the game, and there was rush hour traffic. My father looked at the bumper-to-bumper traffic and he said, "Everybody is coming to see Mex peetch."

My father, Samuel H. Patkin (I never found out what the "H" stood for), had come from Russia with my mother Rebecca. I never saw him naked. Never saw him without his toupee. They had relatives in Philadelphia, which is why he settled there.

He worked as a night clerk for a while, downtown, in a hotel that was one notch above a flophouse. And then, one of his cousins talked him into opening a delicatessan, even though he didn't know salami from sandpaper, and he had no idea how to keep inventory. The deli was on the corner of 7th and Dudley, which is where I was born. Soon after, we moved to 58th and Rodman, a neighborhood made famous many years later, when the cops dropped an incendiary bomb atop the MOVE headquarters, and an entire block burned to the ground.

My dad never really learned to read and write English. He figured things out phonetically after a while, which is why my Navy buddies loved it when I got mail from home. He'd start out writing, "Deer Mex," and he always closed the letter, "Your fater, Sam."

I was a tough kid in a tough neighborhood, but the most meaningful day of my childhood came on a trip to the ballpark sponsored by the synagogue.

We sat in a musty corner of Shibe Park, watching the Philadelphia Athletics. Jimmy Foxx, he became my hero. I idolized him. I remember seeing Ty Cobb play. I saw Eddie Collins play. I fell in love with the game and somehow I got an A's cap, which I wore every hour of the day.

When it came time to go to bed, I'd stick it under my pillow.

My father was on the road all the time, so it was my mother's job to discipline the kids. She did her best, but she was easy-going, and I took advantage of that. My father would come home, she'd tell him about the mischievous things I'd done, he'd whip out the belt, whack me a few times. Sometimes, after really bad episodes, he'd use the buckle.

Once I started pitching, my father encouraged me. Brought me juice, thought that would help my strength. He never really understood the game—only that the crowd loved it when I whiffed someone. So he'd holler, "Strike him out, Mex" at the top of his lungs.

In those days, when I wasn't pitching, I played third base. One game, our starting pitcher was getting belted around. My father came walking out of the stands, onto the field, out to the mound. He walked up to the pitcher, grabbed the baseball, walked over to third, and handed it to me. "Here," he said, "you peetch."

The psychologists can probably figure out why I acted up and acted out so much—absent father, on the road so much, craving for attention, all that razzmatazz. Me, I grew up skinny, homely, with a big nose, a long neck, a narrow waist and a small cap size. I was the homeliest guy on the block. My nickname was "Big Nose." To me, ugly was a four-letter word.

I'm still that way. I hate it when guys walk up to me now, introduce me to someone and say, "Isn't he ugly?"

Maybe they figure, because I'm a clown, they can't hurt my feelings. Maybe they think I will come back with some funny remark. I'm not "on" all the time. I don't think someone who is "on" all the time is funny. I think he's sick.

My parents didn't think I was ugly. They entered me and my brother, Eddie, in a beautiful baby contest on the boardwalk in Wildwood one year. Put us in a double carriage. Now, when I talk about it, I say our noses went past the judges' stand, and 10 minutes later, the carriage went by. We didn't win anything.

I guess I suffered from sibling rivalry, although I never knew it at the time. The kids on the block were always encouraging me and Eddie to fight. So, we'd get out on the sidewalk and we'd spar, swapping punches, slaps. One time, Eddie had had enough and he started to run away. I yelled for him to stop, but he wouldn't. I grabbed a rock and heaved it... Bang! caught him right in the back of the head. He needed two stitches to close the wound.

Things got a little hairier the day I found a gun in my father's dresser drawer. It was left over from the days he worked as a night clerk at that hotel. Kept it wrapped in wax paper. I guess I was about 10 at the time. I grabbed the gun, pointed it at Eddie and pretended to pull the trigger.

Eddie didn't think it was funny and he told me to quit. When I wouldn't, he grabbed my arm and yanked it down. In the scuffle, I pulled the trigger and the gun went off. The bullet grazed Eddie's knee, left him with a powder burn on his thigh. It went through the bureau drawer, leaving a small hole, and into the wall behind the bureau, leaving another small hole.

I managed to pry the bullet out of there with a pliers. And because the wood on the bureau drawer wasn't splintered, I guess my father never noticed.

One great thing, my brother never told my father. I don't know what the punishment would have been for that bit of mischief. I know I used to hide his belt when I was due for some punishment. And I'd hide the cat of nine tails (a short wooden stick with strips of leather dangling down) he kept in the closet.

Despite the close call, I never stopped wrestling with my brother. Once, in front of the Bryant Public School, I almost killed him. We were scuffling on a big stoop in front of the building. I shoved him, and he toppled over, landing head first on the sidewalk. I toppled with him, but he broke the fall, and I wasn't hurt. But he was bleeding and was out like a light.

They had to take him to the hospital to sew him up.

Maybe it was all those episodes that caused the neighbors to think of me as a bad kid. I resented the reputation. I brooded about the way they shunned me. The kids in the neighborhood were always welcome in our house, but I was never allowed inside the other kids' homes.

And I never got invited to the birthday parties other kids had. I remember one kid, named Jimmy Biron, and his mother decided to take a bunch of kids to the Tower Theatre. She had two cars full of kids, maybe 15 kids. But not me. I wasn't invited. I hitch-hiked to the theatre and I waited outside. She saw me, took pity on me, and took me inside. But when the movie was over and the other kids were invited back to the house, I still wasn't welcome.

I had my share of street fights. Mostly with the Irish

kids. I had to go through the Irish neighborhood to get to school. The bullies would be waiting for me. I'd try to out-talk them and if that didn't work, I'd try to out-run them. And if that didn't work, I'd stand there and fight. I was a skinny kid, an easy target, and with my big nose, they had no trouble identifying me as "a Hebe."

Times have changed dramatically. There are gangs in Philadelphia, same as in other big cities. But now, gang warfare leaves young people dead in the streets. We had gang fights in those days too, but they didn't involve deadly weapons, no knives, no guns. What we staged were clip fights. We'd nail two pieces of wood together, in the shape of a pistol, and then stretch a rubber band from the front end to a notched back. You'd put a paper clip back there, and the rubber band would propel the clip at your target. It was a kind of unwritten rule that you didn't aim for the eyes. If you wanted a rubber band that would last, you cut strips off old tires.

Another thing we'd like to cut up were the neighbors' hoses. If they left them out at night, we'd slash a piece off to play hose ball. You'd take that two- or three-inch piece of hose and you'd flip it, like a softball pitcher. The batter tried to hit it, swinging a broom handle. You needed a good eye for that.

My sister, Ruth, was four years younger than I was. I was protective of her, more so than Eddie. We'd go to the movies together. She loved the movies. Could name every actor and actress in every movie, right down to the bit parts. We'd sit there and cry at the sad parts. I can still remember *Wings* and a movie called *The Volga Boat Men*. She can still tell you the bit players in every movie.

When I was about 10, I had a scary episode with a pervert. I was at the State Theatre when this man came and sat in the seat next to me. He started whispering to me, and then he said he'd give me a dime if I let him hold my "thing."

A dime? That was big money then. I didn't understand what he was up to, but he gave me a dime and put his hand inside my pants. Kept it there until the movie ended.

Then he said he'd like to pay my way into the Nixon Theatre, which was nearby. I told him I had to get home.

I ran home, told my father what had happened. He called the police. They came, asked for a description of the man. Hey, it was dark, it was a movie theatre, I was a kid, I couldn't give them any kind of description.

My father warned me against letting that ever happen again. The memory stayed with me. It probably helps explain why I'm homophobic.

I kept acting up in school, although I really liked geography. I was good at drawing maps. I'd draw the map, remember where the country belonged. I was good at spelling, but terrible at algebra. Mrs. Wheatly was my algebra teacher. She hated me.

I once got a letter from my history teacher. She saw a write-up about me in the paper, wrote me, said she was proud of what I'd accomplished.

In eighth grade, I had to attend summer school to get enough credits to go to high school. In high school, I had to go to summer school three times. Was that a record?

I might have been the only athlete at West Philadelphia High School to flunk gym. The gym teacher didn't like me. I clowned around too much. He once gave me a VVVP rating. That stands for very, very, very poor. His name was Ben Stakowsky. He played at Temple, then taught at West Philadelphia High.

I even flunked music and that ain't easy. I'm not sure why. I think I sang falsetto during assembly.

My father saw me wearing that baseball cap all the time, getting lousy grades in school, and said, "You're a bum."

In high school I tried football, Pop Warner League. I got my collarbone broken in a game in Phoenixville. We ran an end-around play, I was wearing a pair of drugstore shoulder pads. A guy hit me high, busted my collarbone. They patched me up at Misericordia Hospital. I never played football again.

I started out as an outfielder, a third baseman. And

then, in gym class one day, I threw my leg higher than anybody in baseball. The gym teacher was also the coach. He liked me reaching back, thought I had great leverage.

He said, "You ought to be a pitcher."

At West Philadelphia High School I was second team. And then, last game of the season, the varsity went on strike because someone had been kicked off the team. We were playing Overbrook, the school Wilt Chamberlain made famous, a tough rival. Played them at 49th and Haverford, in front of a big crowd.

The coach turned to me, and said, "Max, you're gonna pitch."

Let's face it, I don't think he had anybody else available. I pitch, strike out 15, we win the game. Muggs Groff, who coached the Brown Prep team, was there. What I called the dummies, guys who were not college material as scholars, went to Brown Prep to get credits that would help them get scholarships.

I thought that if I went to Brown Prep I could get enough credits to qualify for a baseball scholarship at Temple. Pep Young, the Temple baseball coach, had seen me pitch, and he wanted me. I went to Brown Prep for two years, lost only one game while I was there. I knew I wasn't the college type. I was the only guy who flunked study hall in high school. For a while, the only book I read was one of those eight-page dirty comic books, starring Moon Mullins. X-rated stuff. I got caught with one once, the principal kept it.

I beat every college freshman team we played. Pitched against Tex Warrington, who went on to play football at Auburn. Beat him, 1–0. Pitched against Admiral Farragut and struck out 22, but lost in 11 innings. I could throw hard, but I was wild, so I scared the wit out of everyone. They didn't dare dig in on me.

I was tall, so I made the basketball team at Brown Prep too. I couldn't handle the ball, but all they wanted out of their center was rebounds, and I was a decent rebounder. Best game I ever played in my life was against the Villanova freshmen. In those days, you didn't play varsity ball as a freshman. And Villanova had this blue-chip prospect named Art Spector. Years later, he played with the Celtics. I scored 14 points that game, hit six shots from the corner, with Spector covering me. I ran out of gas that game. I hadn't played that much and I was puffing like a steam engine. At halftime, they were treating me like a god, begging me to keep it up.

But I got tired, wound up fouling out.

I also pitched for the McCall Post, in Legion ball. We lost the state championship game at the Baker Bowl in '36. Johnny Stevens was the umpire, the first year for him. A guy stole home in the 10th inning for the winning run. To this day, every time I see Johnny, who went on to be a big league umpire, I yell, "the guy was out."

I pitched for an amateur team named Wentz-Olney that was good enough to play an exhibition game against the A's. Elmer Valo, who made it to the big leagues, was a teammate. I even pitched against Grover Cleveland Alexander, the legendary pitcher. They made a movie about his life once, and a guy named Ronald Reagan played Alexander—wonder whatever became of that actor? Alexander was finished with his big league career and he was making token appearances for the House of David team. He'd pitch to the leadoff hitter, and then go sit in the dugout.

I pitched that day, beat them, 1–0.

My first pro tryout was a disaster. A scout for Cincinnati got me a tryout with the Reds. He brought me out there.

They let me throw batting practice. I'm throwing pretty good and they're hitting me pretty good. They've got guys like Ernie Lombardi, Bucky Walters. Now, Hank Gowdy, the Cincy pitching coach, yells at me, "Hey, kid, you're not standing on the mound right."

I tell him my high school coach said I had good form. What did I know?

Gowdy tells me to go out to centerfield and shag flies. I tell him, I'm a pitcher, what am I gonna do out there? But I borrow a hat from a guy named Nino Bongiovanni. He was the only guy with a hat, size 6 5/8, that fit me.

When the workout ended, I stuck the hat in my duffel bag and walked away. The next day, the scout calls me, says, "Where's the hat?"

The ballclub was so cheap in those days, each guy only had one hat.

I lied, told him I didn't have it. Years later, Bill McKechnie, who managed that Cincy team, was a coach for Cleveland when I joined the club. He grabbed a bat, chased me around the clubhouse, screaming, "You big-nosed son of a bitch, we had to send for a new hat."

I also had a tryout with the Phillies. Hans Lobert was the manager. They had a terrible team. I'm a silly looking kid, 33-inch sleeve, 14-inch neck, a 29-inch waist. They're all laughing at me. Chuck Klein hits a line drive that slams into my foot. I'm jumping around and they're yelling, "Be a dog, kid, be a dog." So, I start barking in pain. I could barely walk, let alone pitch.

A Dodgers scout brought me in for a tryout. Leo Durocher was there. I remember how crazy it all seemed. The National Guard guys were there, with their rifles, as the color guard. Durocher asked the guys if they had any live ammo. He stuck a bullet in a rifle and chased players around the clubhouse, telling them he was gonna shoot them in the ass.

Scared the hell out of everybody.

I was pitching for Stonehurst when a Red Sox scout came to watch me. I pitched a terrific game that day, maybe a three- or four-hitter. He signed Bill Peterman, my catcher. Years later, he told me I didn't have a chance, because the Red Sox were not going to sign a Jewish player. I don't know whether to believe that or not, because they did have Moe Berg.

I didn't get discouraged. I knew I could pitch. I knew I could throw hard.

The White Sox offered me a tryout. They had me throwing to Skeets Dickey, Bill's brother, on the sidelines. Everybody was laughing at me, because he seemed to be throwing the ball back as hard as I was throwing it to him.

I must have made a decent impression, because they

gave me a contract to pitch for Waterloo, Iowa. Spring training camp was in Jonesboro, Arkansas. They must have had a hundred guys there.

I bought myself a rubber jacket because I'd seen Johnny Mize wear one once. It's 105 degrees and I'm sweating bullets and someone asks me why I've got a rubber jacket on? I knew it was a mistake, but I didn't want to throw it away. The general manager there was Joe Brown Jr., the son of the famous Joe E. Brown, who played a lot of comic parts in baseball movies. Maybe he didn't like my face, or my body, or the way I leaned in for the signs like I was going to topple over. Whatever, he sold my contract for $100.

I was assigned to Wisconsin Rapids in the Wisconsin State League.

This was 1941, and I might have led the league in wild pitches.

I started off 3–1, but I wound up 10–8. Struck out 134 guys in 178 innings, which is good. But I also walked 95, threw 13 wild pitches and hit nine batters.

I also scored one knockout, a sportswriter. The press box was behind home plate, about 15 feet off the ground. I let one go and it got away from me. Took off, over the batter's head, over the umpire's head. It zips into the press box and it hits the back wall. It bounces back and it nails the back of this writer's head, knocking him cold.

From then on, whenever I pitched, the writers kept the screen in front of the box closed.He forgave me, and later on, he became publicity director for the White Sox.

I remember one day when the Oshkosh team came in. Hank Bauer was going to pitch against me. (How's that for a piece of trivia?) They drive in on their bus and the players ask if there's a whore house in town. I tell them there's one on the outskirts of town. They get the bus driver to drive 12 of them out there. Me, I just sat on the bus, because I knew I was pitching that night. The whole dozen guys went in, plus the bus driver.

That night, they were loose as ashes and I was tight and they beat the hell out of me. I probably would have had trouble getting the bus driver out that night.

I hit another crossroads in Green Bay—ballpark with the backstop right behind home plate. I was pitching, man on second, I throw a wild pitch. The man from second tries to score. It was their outfielder, named Sweed Hansen, a good ballplayer, biggest guy I ever saw in my life. He's charging around third and my catcher, Frank Comiskey, is sauntering after the ball. He picks it up, throws it on the third base side of the plate. I dive for the ball, the runner slides into my arm.

I went back out there, tried to throw, but the pain was too much.The team did not have an orthopedic doctor assigned to it, so they sent me back to Wisconsin Rapids to get it checked. I wound up hitch-hiking to Wausau to get it X-rayed. They told me I had bone chips near the ulnar nerve and they wanted to operate. When I balked, they released me.

The Green Bay team knew I had some talent, a good arm, so they took a chance and signed me. They had a shot at the pennant. The first game I pitched in for Green Bay was against Wisconsin Rapids and the crowd really got on me, booing me. They thought I had maneuvered to get with a better club.

I beat them, throwing mostly curve balls. I pitched a couple more times, but I couldn't throw hard.

On days when I didn't pitch, I coached first base. My manager was Frank Parenti and he wanted me to get on the guys on the other team. I'd needle them. I'd get on their starting pitcher, telling him he wouldn't last two innings. The other guys hated it. They weren't used to bench jockeying. Some guys would grab me on the street, threaten me. But they knew when I pitched against them, that ball in my hand was a lethal weapon.

And then I got into an argument with Deacon Delmar, the pitching coach—I think it was over shagging flies. They fired me. During the playoffs. But the war was heating up, and I was soon headed in a different direction, towards the South Pacific.

Chapter 4

A WRECK SALVAGED BY VEECK

They gave me a night in Wilkes-Barre. That's all they gave me. The night.

Mike McNally, the general manager, suggested it to Dick Porter, the manager. They said it would be "Max Patkin Night," so I invite my mother, my father, my brother, my sister...

The night before, they had maybe 400 people in the ballpark, 500 tops. My night, it's standing room only. We're playing the Hartford team, fighting for second place. Scranton won the pennant by 15 games that year, but we're scrambling for second.

Porter says, "Let's pitch Max, it's his night." He asks me how my arm feels and I tell him it's okay, but still bothering me a little.

I go out there, full house, and before I throw the first pitch, I glance down at the bullpen and they've got a guy warming up. That's a great way to instill confidence.

I pitch the whole game, we win 6–5. Everybody is saying, "What a wonderful night, what did they give you, Max?"

And I have to tell them they didn't give me anything. Lenny Brader, a dear friend of mine, felt so sorry for me he gave me a pair of shoes.

McNally hears about it, calls me in, says, "I understand people are talking about why we didn't give you anything. I'll tell you what I'm gonna give you, I'm gonna give you your release. You can't pitch anymore."

Before that, on the road, he'd called me in, told me I ought to be a comedian because Al Schacht was coming to the end of his career. I argued, told him I could still throw pretty good.

I was deceiving myself. That spring, coming north, I pitched in an exhibition game on a damp, cool night. I hurt something in my shoulder. Pop Savage was the trainer. He told me, "Max, as loose as you are, just work it out." But I knew I had torn something and I would never throw hard again.

McNally said I didn't throw hard enough anymore and that I had no future as a pitcher. It almost broke my heart.

And then he told me that the Harrisburg club, Cleveland's Class B farm team, was playing an exhibition against the Philadelphia Athletics. He told me to come with him to Harrisburg, that he'd talk to Les Bell, the Harrisburg manager, and he'd let me do my routine.

I remember Connie Mack, who owned the A's, was there, sitting in the stands. The A's were kicking the hell out of Harrisburg and I went out to clown. The act was raw, I was still figuring out what made people laugh. I glanced over and Connie Mack was hysterical, shaking with laughter. He was such a staid old guy, starched collar, straw hat, but he was tittering, trying to hide his mouth with his hand.

I was a hit, got great write-ups. For years and years, Earl Mack, Connie's son, would pull me over to his father and say, "Dad, this is the guy who made you laugh in Harrisburg."

We've got a split doubleheader against Scranton on Memorial Day. One game in the afternoon, drive back to Wilkes-Barre for sandwiches, then back to Scranton.

Bob Kuzava is going to start the night game. I tell Porter, I'd like to pitch, if there's a spot, because I think I can still throw. Kuzava gets knocked out in the third inning. They put me in the ballgame. I've already walked past the Scranton dugout and asked the manager if they could use a pitcher. He had nine guys on that team go up to the big leagues, including Sam Mele and Mel Parnell. He just laughed at me.

I get in the game and I can't get anybody out. So, in desperation, I put on my act. Mele is the hitter. I put the baseball down and I pick up the rosin bag. Mele steps out, laughing. He says, "I can't hit against this silly so-and-so. I throw the rosin bag at him. They took me out after an inning and a half.

That was it. The fat lady sang, it was over.

I finished my pro career over .500, and how many pitchers can say that?

A man named Ray Nemec sent me my complete record. He does that for a hobby, keeps track of the careers of guys who never get to the majors. He wondered why, in some places, the year of my birth showed up as 1922, and in others, 1920.

I was born in 1920, but when I got out of the Navy I probably told some baseball people I was born in '22, because I didn't think they'd give a 26-year-old a real chance.

My record looked like this:

Year	Club	League	G	CG	IP	W	L	PCT	H	BB	SO	R
41	Wisconsin Rapids	Wisc St	27	13	178	10	8	.556	170	95	134	94
42	Wis.Rapids/G. Bay	Wisc St	13	3	65	3	4	.429	59	39	32	27
43/45	(United States Navy)											
46	Wilkes-Barre	Eastern	5	1	19	1	1	.500	19	12	7	15

I get released. And I go home to Philadelphia.

I get a call from Dave Kohn, the general manager in Harrisburg. He wants me to come to Harrisburg and do my routine during an exhibition game they're playing against Cleveland, the parent club. He offers me $100, I accept. I go down there, do the same show, it goes over terrific, except that I tear a ligament in my knee. I was coaching first and I threw my leg up in the air. Threw it so high, it ripped my knee.

Soon after, I get a call from Bill Veeck, who had just bought the Cleveland team. He said that Lou Boudreau had said some nice things about me, and he wanted me to come to Cleveland to talk. Veeck loved the game. The comedy, the midget, the exploding scoreboards—that was icing on the cake to him. I get to Cleveland and he tells me he's going to bring in Jackie Price, from Oakland, as a pre-game act, and he wants me to perform before the game, too.

Boudreau interrupts and says he wants me to coach for two innings of every ballgame. He says I'll drive the other team nuts.

Veeck asks me what I was making at Wilkes-Barre and I tell him $350 a month.

He says, "I'll double it, I'll give you $650."

(I add $350 and $350, that's more than $650. But I don't give a damn. I'm so happy, I'd have worked for peanuts.)

I tell him about my knee and how it will take a month to get better. Then I sign a contract for the lowest amount in the history of baseball—one dollar. I've got a personal services contract for the $650 a month, all year 'round, and a baseball contract for a dollar.

A month later, I join the Cleveland club. It's a Sunday afternoon, and I'm going to make my first appearance in front of 80,000 people, standing room only. I'd like to say it was because of me, but it wasn't. They were honoring Babe Ruth, Ty Cobb and Tris Speaker that day. Al Schacht was there. He had been booked by the previous owner. Veeck didn't really want him, but a deal's a deal. Schacht was out there, doing his pre-game stuff, big glove, top hat, tuxedo. And Babe Ruth, in the dugout, says, "I hate that son of a bitch."

And then he hollers over to Mel Harder, who was the pitching coach. "Mel, you want to throw to me?" Ruth was in civilian clothes, his voice hoarse from the throat cancer.

Harder says he'll throw and he looks around and says, "Who wants to catch?" Jim Hegan says he'll catch. Ruth takes off his jacket and walks out there. It was the last time Babe Ruth ever batted in his life.

He rolled up his sleeves, rolled up his pants, put my shoes on that he'd borrowed.

Harder ran out to the mound, Hegan put on the catcher's gear and went behind home plate. And here came Babe, with four bats. He tossed three aside. I'd never heard such applause in my life. Schacht just walked off the field.

Now, Harder pitches to Babe and he's taking feeble swings. Hits a few weak grounders. He's swinging from the heels, trying to hit it out of the park. I guess he took eight or nine swings. I remember him walking back to the dugout, dragging the bat, everyone had tears in their eyes. Everyone knew he was dying of cancer.

Then the game started and I was shaking in my shoes. My first game in the big leagues and there's 80,000 in the ballpark. Boudreau wanted me to work the first two innings, get me out of the way, before the game got close.

I did two innings, got the laughs. By the time we went on the road, to Detroit, we were already being written up as Bill Veeck's circus.

I remember, in Detroit, Hank Greenberg was playing first. I ask him, "Can you do this little Jew boy a favor? As you're tossing the ball around, can I make out like I'm giving you a hot-foot?"

He says, "Okay, I'll be your stooge."

He had this habit of keeping his foot on the bag, while he stretched before each inning. I go out there, light a whole book of matches, toss it aside. Now, I take another match book, I'm on my hands and knees, pretending to stick it in his heel. He jumps up and down, like he's been burned. Then he grabs me by the shirt, picks me off the ground, shakes me. It went over great.

I had seen Schacht back in 1941, when I was with the Wisconsin Rapids. I remember that he was a funny guy. I even remember telling a guy in the dugout, "That man makes a million a year." He was probably making $100 a game at the time, but I'm not a Harvard graduate, and math was never my best subject.

Years later, Schacht was involved in one of my tougher nights. Some friends of mine had contacted him before he did a performance at Valley Forge General Hospital. They wanted him to take a look at me, and he said he'd do it at Valley Forge. They were playing the Phillies in an exhibition and it was standing room only. Schacht did his pre-game routine. He was working alone then. Nick Altrock had worked with him down through the years. Worked with him, but they never got along, never spoke.

I come out in the fourth inning and I'm wearing a Valley Forge uniform. Nobody's laughing. I'm knocking my brains out and nobody's laughing. I spread-eagle my legs, stick my nose to the ground, steal the catcher's signals, nothing. I know what gets laughs, and now I'm baffled. I'm out there two innings, same reaction, nothing. I'm disgusted.

I walk off, my friends come down to see me. I ask them what happened. They say, "You dumb son-of-a-gun, the worst thing you could have done was put on that Valley Forge Hospital uniform. They thought you were a psycho. They didn't know you were a clown.

"If you were a guy out of the mental ward, they didn't know whether to laugh or to cry."

Here I thought I was giving one of my best performances and it turned out to be one of my worst.

Schacht was known as "The Clown Prince of Baseball" then. It's not like you can copyright something like that. When he died, I became "The Clown Prince of Baseball."

It's a small kingdom. I'm the only one out there. And when I go, nobody will move into that slot. The travel is too punishing, the pay too skimpy, the life too lonely.

In the early days, there were other acts out there. Johnny Jones, he used trick bats that would explode. A guy named Murray O'Flynn had a pre-game act. He'd come out of a teepee, but that's all I remember about him. Sometimes, a whole team got in on it. The Indianapolis Clowns were great. Goose Tatum played first base for them. He was the funniest man I'd ever seen. The House of David played at Bushwick Park in Brooklyn. All the guys wore beards. They'd do the phantom infield, throw an invisible ball around the diamond, play a high-speed game of pepper.

King Tut was out there. And a midget named Specs Bebop.

Now, you've got the Chicken, who started in San Diego. I'm not jealous of the Chicken, just envious. I know he's cheap. He'll stiff the clubhouse guys or he'll give them a doll. I always tip the clubhouse guy, and I'm making a lot less than the Chicken.

The first time I ever saw the Chicken, I was sitting in owner Roy Kroc's box in San Diego. The general manager said to me, "Wait until you see this act." Suddenly, there he was, in the centerfield bleachers, shaking his feathers. He came down on the field, did his stuff, paraded through the stands. He was funny. I made one of the biggest mistakes I ever made, in 1986, agreeing to appear in the same ballpark with the Chicken. A. Ray Smith, the Louisville owner, was determined to draw a million fans that year. So he signed me and the Chicken to appear at the first three games of the season, against Buffalo.

They did a story the day before and the Chicken sounded so humble, so polite, saying that I had seniority, and that whatever I wanted to do was okay with him. We get to the ballpark, I'm in the clubhouse and the Chicken's manager says to me, "Max, you'll go out there in the seventh inning." I argue. He says the Chicken will work the third, fourth and fifth. I argue some more.

I storm out of there, looking for A. Ray Smith. I tell him what's going on and he says, "Max, I hate to tell you this, but Kentucky Fried Chicken is sponsoring the Chicken's appearance, they're paying him a lot of money, and he's got the run of the ballpark."

I'm really hissed now, and I ask why he didn't tell me that when he booked me, and he says, lamely, he forgot.

I'm ready to walk out, but I think about it, for about 20 seconds, and I agree to go on.

The game starts, they've got 25,000 in the stands on a cool, April night. He goes out there in the third inning, does his bit, and the fans love him. By the time I go out there, in the seventh inning, the home team is losing, 9–0. How many people do you think were left in that ballpark? Maybe 3,000. I get a smattering of applause. So I come in, grab the leather bag of baseballs in the dugout, and start throwing the balls into the stands.

Jim Fregosi is managing and he's going nuts. Those were the game balls and he's screaming at me. I'm screaming back. I must have tossed two dozen balls into the seats before they stopped me.

I went out, did the eighth inning, and heard more noise in a library. the Chicken just wasn't fair to me, and that's why I don't have too many kind words to say about him.

Louisville drew 70,000 for the three games. The Buffalo general manager, Bob Belonni, must have been impressed. He booked me for a game in Buffalo late in the season. The week before the date, he calls me, says he'd like to cancel. They were in contention for a playoff spot, and I think a lump was forming in his throat.

I squawked and finally he said, "I'll book you next year."

For the next seven years, he never got around to booking me. He won't even answer the phone. Puts his secretary on. She says he's in conference. How many conferences does that cheap sucker go to?

There's one more postscript to the appearance with the Chicken. Louisville broke the million mark and A. Ray Smith invited us back. They had more Hall of Famers at the party than anywhere outside of Cooperstown. Maybe 25 Hall of Famers. Al Hirt played. Phil Harris sang. Stan Musial got up and played his harmonica. I was out there dancing, putting on my act and here came a cop. He handcuffs me, drags me off the floor. I ask what the charge is and he says, "Indecent dancing!"

I look around and A. Ray Smith is giggling. He put the cop up to it.

Mr. Dyn-o-mite is out there. Blows himself up at second base. Tough act, even though it only lasts two seconds. He can hardly hear anybody now.

I've worked with Morganna, the stripper, who made a

name for herself as baseball's kissing bandit. She'd jiggle onto the field and run up to a player and smooch him.

I worked with her once, in Jacksonville. Bobby Bragan Jr. was the general manager there. She was working in a nightclub in Jacksonville, and she came out to the ballpark wearing a white top.

I'm coaching first, and I'm filthy, from crawling around in the basepaths. She's supposed to run out and kiss the pitcher, and I'm supposed to plant one on her as she goes by. She gets to the baseline, I grab her, and as I'm holding her, she's so top-heavy, she falls. I fall right on top of her—it was like a trampoline, I bounce right up. She hears the television crews coming, so she grabs me, and kisses me. I don't know, I'm not sure that's a family act.

Chapter 5

THE PRICE WAS RIGHT

I had a Cleveland contract for a buck, and it wasn't long before I got the Indians a million dollars worth of publicity. Most of it bad.

We were playing a game against the Red Sox, in League Park, in '46. That was the year the Red Sox won the pennant. I'm coaching first, Les Fleming was the hitter, and Cal Hubbard was behind the plate. He calls a pitch a strike, and I rub my hand across my neck to indicate I thought the pitch was high. Hubbard steps out from behind the plate, points at me, and says, "You're gone!"

Lou Boudreau, who was the player-manager, rushes out to argue. Hubbard tells him, "I can't stand to look at that silly son of a bitch any more."

The Indians protest, Bill Veeck sends a letter to the league president, Will Harridge. I remember when Harridge once introduced me to his wife. I said, "My nose is bigger than she is." The whole thing becomes a big issue. It gets written up in The Sporting News. Columnists are taking sides. Bob Burnes in St. Louis wrote an editorial saying I had no business in baseball, that I made a mockery of the game. It was a terrible story.

I took it to Veeck and he said, "What's your problem?"

I told him it was a terrible review of my act. And he said, "Max, did they spell your name right?"

He taught me that as long as they're writing about you, the public is aware of you. And that's why I never stiff a reporter. I always find time. And, down through the years, I could count the number of negative stories written about me on my fingers—well, maybe my fingers and my toes.

In his book, *Veeck as in Wreck*, Bill remembered the

reaction of the umpires: "The umpires viewed him with mixed emotions," Veeck wrote. "They couldn't stop themselves from laughing at him, and yet they had to keep an eye on him because he was the only man who could dispute a call with a twitch of a muscle.

"After one of our boys had been called out on strikes, Max would sometimes topple over on his back, as rigidly as a falling tree, as if he were fainting from the shock of it all.

"He once arose to find big Cal Hubbard bearing down on him to throw him out of the game, and that can be a shock. What made it tough for Max was that the umpire on first base would sometimes be saying, 'Come on, Max, do that backward fall before you go,' while the umpire-in-chief was scowling down to warn him off."

It didn't take long for the big leaguers to start messing with me. One cool September evening, I was coaching first base against Washington. Bill McGowan was umpiring first base. I was still doing that bit where I kick off my shoe, smell it, pretend to faint. I'm sprawled there and someone is supposed to come out with a bucket of water to revive me. Only the guys had mixed flour with the water, turned it into a paste.

Here comes Mickey Vernon with the bucket, throws the glop all over me. The whole coaching box turned white. McGowan stares at me and says, "You've gotta clean that up." I'm on my hands and knees, with towels, trying to soak up the paste. And now, my uniform is hardening up. The stuff is turning into plaster and I'm stiff as a board and the crowd loves it.

To this day, whenever I see Cal Griffith, he says his father, who owned the Washington club, never laughed so hard in his life as he did that day.

I remember my first trip into New York with the Indians. I remember Tiny Bonham was going to pitch against Bob Feller. Bobby Riggs played an exhibition tennis match against Jack Kramer before the game. Phil Rizzuto came up to me and he told me that Frank Crosetti had a great sense of humor, told me he loved my act.

In those days the players left their gloves on the field between innings. Rizzuto told me that Crosetti always picked up the third baseman's glove on his way to the coach's box and that he'd spin it, out of habit. Rizzuto told me to run behind Crosetti, imitate him, that he'd get a big kick out of it.

Sounded fine to me. I get out there, fall in behind Crosetti, copying the way he ran. He realizes what's happening, bends down, picks up the glove, wheels around, and swats me right across the nose with the glove. I'm so stunned, I topple over, backwards. I reach up, there's blood pouring out of my nose. Rizzuto laughed the whole inning.

The first time we played in St. Louis, Jack Kramer wasn't too happy with my antics, coaching first. The Indians are pounding Kramer, we've got a man on first, and I'm doing my stuff, pretending to steal signs. Kramer wheels, and instead of trying to pick the guy off first, he throws right at my head. I hit the deck, get up, and shake myself like a golden retriever coming out of the water. Everyone laughed. Except Kramer. Meanwhile the runner had scampered to second. I understood what Kramer was thinking. You show me a good loser and I'll show you a bleeping idiot.

I'd be out there for two innings and it didn't take long to develop a following. Which was fine for me, but tough on Buster Mills, the coach who came out to follow me. It was okay at home, but on the road, the fans really gave him a hard time. I'd finish my two innings and Buster would trot out there and they'd be screaming at him, "What are you doing out there? We want Patkin."

He was an easy-going guy and I sympathized with him.

I was in the big leagues, even though it was as a comic-coach, and the whole thing was an adventure. Rooming with Jackie Price just added to the excitement.

Price was an above-average shortstop, playing in Oakland. But he could also do phenomenal things with baseballs. He could throw three baseballs at the same time, one to a guy standing on second, the other two to guys standing on opposite sides of the mound. He could unzip his fly and catch an 80 MPH pitch in his pants. Or he'd unbutton his shirt and catch it with his stomach. He could bat, using the knob of the bat. He'd stand there and bunt the ball with the knob. Got his nose broken a few times from foul tips, got his fingers mashed a few times.

When he performed, he'd drive around the outfield in a Jeep and Jim Hegan would hit fungoes (Hegan was a great fungo hitter) and Jackie would drive under them and catch them with one hand. Later, when Price went on the road, he bought a bazooka to fire the baseballs into the air and then he'd drive to the spot and catch them. He could hang upside down and hit pitches. He'd put his feet in straps from the bar of a swing set and he'd hit. He was amazing.

He could also drink a case of beer a day. And his affection for snakes could cause problems. I know, because I roomed with him. He'd keep the snakes in a drawer, and he once scared a chambermaid so bad, the owner threw the team out of the hotel.

Some of his teammates weren't thrilled with Price's passion for snakes. Don Black was deathly afraid of them. And once, Price slipped one of his snakes into the shower. Black thought it was a belt, bent down to pick it up. It started moving and Black bolted out of the shower, looking for Price, ready to strangle him. Sometimes, Price took the snake out onto the field with him, tucked in his shirt. Once, a runner slid into second, and the snake poked his head out of Price's shirt. The guy jumped off the bag and Price tagged him out.

The Indians trained in Tucson in those days. And Price went too far on a West Coast exhibition trip. We were touring with the White Sox, sharing the same train from Los Angeles to San Diego. There just happened to be a carload of women bowlers on the train too. A bunch of us, from both teams, were kidding around with the women, and here came Jackie...

He slides a snake onto the floor and the women start screaming.

Some of them are hanging onto the baggage racks, standing on the seats. The conductor hears them, comes looking for Boudreau. When we got to San Diego, Price gets kicked off the club. There were headlines in the papers, asking if we were running a ballclub or a circus. I was afraid I'd get fired too, but I didn't. Not right away.

Bill Veeck was amazing. He'd had a rough time in the war, lost his leg. Smoked a lot, handled his beer better than anybody I've ever seen, would read a book in one sitting, could talk about any subject.

He was an equal opportunity employer. The first ballclub he wanted to buy was the Phillies. He was going to integrate the team, and that was years before Branch Rickey signed Jackie Robinson. Robinson broke the major league color barrier in 1947 when he played for the Dodgers. That year, Veeck signed Larry Doby, first black player in the American League. Veeck felt it was the right thing to do, but he also had his eye on attendance. He was a baseball man, a promoter, a good human being.

He'd bought Doby's contract from the Newark Bears. Larry was very different from Robinson, who was a fiery, aggressive ballplayer. Once Jackie established himself, he never backed down from anything or anyone. Doby had a different personality. You could see he could run, he could throw, he had a little bit of power. But he needed work on the fundamentals.

Once, with the bases loaded and nobody out, he tried to steal home and he was tagged out. Boudreau fined him for that, and might have even suspended him for a game.

In his book, *The Hustler's Handbook* Veeck wrote about that play. "I can remember a game," Veeck wrote, "when my dear friend Larry Doby tried to steal home against the

Yankees, in a ridiculous situation, and I stated publicly that it was a stupid play.

"Because it was. But that didn't make him stupid, because he's not. I just wanted to know what had got into him. You can understand why stupid people do stupid things; it is always difficult to understand why a bright man does a stupid thing."

Another time, Doby misjudged a ball in the outfield and it hit him on the head.

It wasn't easy, being a pioneer. And I'll never forget the day Rogers Hornsby walked into our clubhouse. Veeck had used him as a hitting instructor in spring training. Hornsby walks in, says in a loud voice, "Imagine that, they're bringing black so-and-so's into the big leagues."

Doby was sitting right there. We all knew he'd heard him. It was just a nasty thing to do.

In the late 70's, Veeck hired Doby to manage the White Sox. Frank Robinson had become the first black manager in Cleveland. But Doby didn't seem to have the personality needed to handle the players he had to manage. Eventually, Veeck had to fire Doby. Called it the toughest decision he ever had to make.

Thinking about that episode brings to mind one of the saddest events in baseball of the last decade, when Al Campanis did that late night interview that led to his firing as general manager of the Dodgers.

I knew Campanis for many years. I know he worked with Jackie Robinson when Robinson played in Montreal. I feel, in my heart, he is not a bigot. But that night, sitting alone, with an ear-piece in his ear, answering questions from Ted Koppel, he said that perhaps black people lacked "the necessities" to manage in the big leagues. Koppel came back from a commercial and gave him the chance to retract, but Al just buried himself.

The Dodgers dumped him, which wasn't fair. And then, Al couldn't get another job. At the major league meetings in Florida, one of the writers from the *Miami Herald* did a story about Campanis walking around, hat in hand, looking for a job. I thought the story was cruel, that it just opened old wounds.

Veeck loved a gag, loved a challenge, loved the game. His office door was always open. He didn't have his calls screened by other people—when you called the ballpark for Veeck, he'd pick up the phone.

A gun mount fell on his foot and crushed it at Bouganvilla, in the South Pacific. He used to come down to the clubhouse and soak that foot. They outfitted him with a wooden leg in Cleveland in 1947. One time, we were sitting around, in the dugout—Boudreau, Joe Gordon, George Case, Al Lopez, and myself—and Veeck said, "Max, how about you and I race to the rightfield fence?"

He wanted a 50-yard handicap because of the wooden leg. He wanted to race for $20.

I agree. Batting practice stops. Everybody is watching. In the old days, the fans would show up early to watch batting practice, so we've got some people in the stands.

We race. He beats me. I'm only making $650 a month, so $20 wasn't pocket change.

Now, Bill McKechnie speaks up. He says he's 65 and he wants to race me if I spot him 30 yards. But I had to do it right then, even though I was still puffing from the first race.

We race. I lose.

Now, Oscar Melillo chimes in. I didn't realize he was a championship runner, running backwards. He says he'll give me a 20-yard handicap and race me 50 yards running backwards.

He beats me.

It was fun while it lasted. But, after the start of the '47 season, Veeck saw that the Indians had the makings of a decent ballclub and he didn't need the comedy as a draw. He booked me into the Hollender Hotel in Cleveland as a nightclub act. I was scared. Eddie White was the featured comedian. I did six or seven minutes, a baseball skit, and I'd jitterbug with the band. He booked me for sports shows. I kept matching up with Bobby Riggs, who had a tennis act. I'd hit the ball back and forth, all loosey-goosey, and then he'd play a real match.

That's when I started appearing at minor league ballparks. I had no agent, no public relations staff. I booked myself into ballparks, made my own travel arrangements. Finally, I hired Irv Nahan as my agent, but first, I had Eddie Gottlieb booking me, out of Philadelphia. Gotty was unique. He booked all the black baseball teams in Philadelphia. He later was general manager and part-owner of the Philadelphia Warriors. They say he used to make up the entire NBA schedule, sitting there at Horn & Hardart's, eating a prune danish.

I did a sports show, with Jim Thorpe, the famous football player who once had to give back his Olympic medals because he'd gotten paid a few bucks years earlier as a baseball player. It was Thorpe who gave me the little-bitty glove I still use in my act. It's about as big as a pancake, and just as thick.

I also barnstormed with Bob Feller's All-Stars and with Enos Slaughter's All-Stars. But when Veeck bought the St. Louis Browns in 1951, I was back in the big leagues. Sort of. People said I fit right in with that team, because it was mainly a bunch of clowns.

Once, I managed to convince some of my friends from Philadelphia that I was really important, a big star—and I used a future Hall of Famer named Ted Wiliams in the gag I pulled.

Willie Mersky, George Wolfman, and a couple of friends had been vacationing in California. Now, they were going back to Philadelphia, by way of St. Louis, and wanted to come to see me perform.

The Browns were playing Boston that day, so I grabbed a bunch of kids before the game and I said I'd give them 50 cents apiece, if they went along with my gag.

The visiting clubhouse was down at the end. Their guys had to pass the Browns' clubhouse, which was up a flight of stairs. I could look out the door and see who was going by. So, I told the kids, when the game ended, and Ted Williams came out of the clubhouse, they were supposed to scream, "There's Ted Williams, let's get his autograph." And then, as I came down the steps, they were supposed to yell, "Hey, here comes Max Patkin" and all come running towards me, ignoring Williams.

I hadn't bribed all of the kids, but enough to make an impression. So they stampeded away from Williams to surround me. My friends are standing there, outside the clubhouse, waiting for me, and they're "*qvelling*" which is a Yiddish word for taking pride.

They went back to Philadelphia, they spread the word of how big a star Max Patkin was in St. Louis.

Which was funny, because I was strictly second banana the day Veeck used the midget, Eddie Gaedel as a pinch-hitter.

It happened in August, and Gaedel was supposed to step out of a birthday cake. In typical Bill Veeck style, it was like a three-ring circus. There was a hand-balancing act at first base, a trampoline act at second, a team of jugglers at third, and I had grabbed a lady out of the grandstands and was doing a jitterbug near the pitcher's mound. Gaedel jumped out of the cake, ran to the dugout, and into the clubhouse to wait for his magic moment, in the second game of the doubleheader.

In the clubhouse, before the game, the ballplayers were all needling Gaedel. We were showing him how to stand, how to fake a bunt. We told him that Gene Bearden was pitching for Detroit, that he was wild, threw the knuckleball, that he never knew where the ball was going to go.

You could see he was getting nervous. And then Veeck came in and told him, "If you swing at a pitch, I'll kill you."

We showed him how to step out of the box and tap his spikes with his little bat. The league president, Will Harridge, knew about it. The umpires were told to go along with it. The writers had been tipped off, but somehow there are no movies of the whole stunt, just still pictures.

The game starts, and the announcer says, "Ladies and gentlemen, batting for Frank Saucier, number one-eighth, Eddie Gaedel."

Leadoff hitter, Saucier had once led the Texas League in hitting. And now, he's out for a pinch-hitter. Here comes Gaedel out of the dugout, with a bunch of little bats on his shoulder.

There were 18,000 people there, a big crowd for the Browns. I used to get laughs there yelling to the fans that I had more people at my house for dinner the night before.

Now, Gaedel gets to the batter's box, and the plate ump, Ed Hurley, whips off his mask, and hollers, "No way."

But Zack Taylor, who was managing the Browns, rushes out of the dugout with a piece of paper. He says it's a genuine big league contract. Red Rolfe was managing Detroit, and he doesn't want any part of it. But Hurley calls Rolfe over, they talk, and Hurley hollers, "Play ball."

Bob Cain was the Detroit pitcher. Gaedel crouches down and his strike zone was about an inch and three-quarters. It was a classic scene.

First pitch, ball one. He steps out, taps his spikes.

He walks on four straight pitches. We wind up loading the bases with nobody out, but we don't score. Who pinch ran for Gaedel? Jimmy Delsing. Good trivia bit.

Vincent X. Flaherty, the fine writer for the *Los Angeles Times*, wrote, "I do not advocate baseball burlesque, such practices do not redound to the better interests of the game, but I claim it was the funniest thing that has happened to baseball in years."

Veeck only paid Gaedel $150 for the gig. He made some more money off public appearances. People tell me he was a bitter guy. Veeck brought him back in '59, when he had the White Sox. Stepped out of a space ship.

Space ship, that was one of the few means of transportation I didn't use down through the years.

Chapter 6

GETTING TO THE PARK ON TIME

Plane, train, bus, cab, limo, I've ridden everything but a blue-nosed mule to make it from one ballpark to another, and never, ever missed a date.

I've had to jump from a burning plane, peel myself out of a car wreck, chase a runaway bus in a beat-up taxi, but somehow I always got to the ballpark on time. The closest call was that Frontier commuter that caught fire going from St. Louis to Little Rock. The hydraulic system started blazing as we came in for the landing at Fayetteville and we had to jump off the plane. They knew I had to get to Little Rock, so they chartered a Piper Cub for me. We get up in the air, the pilot is at least 70 and he puts on an oxygen mask.

He looks over at me and he's mumbling, "I've got a heart condition and asthma."

I say, "H-h-h-h-how long is this f-f-f-f-flight?"

He tells me it's an hour and a half and we're flying over the Ozarks, bouncing around, and I am scared to death.

Meanwhile, he's pointing out the sights. He says, "There's Governor Rockefeller's estate down there."

I tell him, "Keep your eye on the road."

We landed, I kissed that Arkansas ground.

Another close call involved a lot bigger plane, a TWA job out of Philadelphia headed west. We circle the airport five or six times, and finally, the pilot gets on the intercom and says that they can't get the landing gear up, that one of the wheels is stuck. We spend an hour and a half circling and people are starting to get sick, using the barf bags. I'm sitting next to a priest and he's reading the Bible, out loud, in Latin. I knew I was scared when I started to understand him.

Now, they tell us they're heading off-shore, to dump what's left of the gasoline and they'll attempt a belly landing in Pomona, New Jersey. We look out the window, they're laying the foam down.

The stewardess tells us to put our arms up in front of our faces, fasten our seat belts, the whole routine. And then, they tell us they've managed to get the gear fixed manually. We land and they tell us they'll arrange other flights and they'd like to feed us to make up for all the trouble. I don't think anybody wanted that free meal.

When I first started out, I depended on buses and trains to get from town to town. Once, in the early 50's, I'm on my way from Carlsbad, New Mexico, to Fresno, California.

We're out in the desert somewhere, this little out-of-the-way stop and I have to change buses, for one headed to El Paso. I tell the driver, make sure you get my luggage off. I go into this little country store, get a soda, come out, the bus is gone, and no luggage in sight. I'm in this desolate town and my luggage is headed in the wrong direction.

I look around, I spot this dilapidated taxi, like something out of the Toonerville Trolley days. I ask the driver if he can follow the bus. I tell him I'll give him $50. He takes off, we go 20 miles, 30 miles, the cab is starting to overheat, steam comes out of the radiator cap. We catch the bus, pull alongside, the driver waves like he expects us to pass. We finally get him to stop. I chew the driver out, we get my luggage, head back to the crossroads, I get the bus to El Paso, catch a plane to Los Angeles, change for a flight to Fresno and get there, in time to do the show.

El Paso was the scene of another memorable ride, this one involving Charlie Metro, who managed the Cubs for a while. He was a scout then and he was in El Paso, with his son and his son's friend. I told him I was going to Midland next, and he said he had his pickup truck and I could ride with him. It was only a 45-minute flight., and close to a five-hour drive. The temperature was 105 the day before and I wasn't sure I wanted to ride with Charlie.

He told me his truck was air-conditioned, so I said I'd go with him. We get up at six in the morning, the kids scramble into the back and I get up front.

I'm sweating already, so I tell Charlie, "Hey, it's hot, turn on the air-conditioning."

He says, "Roll the window down, Max, that's our air-conditioning." I wanted to jump out right there, but it was 95 degrees and still early in the morning.

We're driving on the Interstate, he's pretty good company, but suddenly I notice, the gas gauge is down to zero. I point it out to Charlie and he says we'll fill it up when we stop for lunch. We pass a sign that says, "Next service station 40 miles." Now I'm really griping, but he waves me off, tells me not to worry about it. Then the needle points to empty. Now I'm desperate. I tell him if we get stuck out here, the rattlesnakes will eat us alive. He's laughing at me and the motor goes chug, chug, chug, like it's dying. I'm out of my head as he pulls over to the side of the road. Then, shazam, he starts it up, and we're on our way again.

How was I to know that that model pickup truck had an auxiliary tank, and all he did was switch it on. He laughed like hell afterwards.

A shorter, but more memorable ride, was the time I went along with Spud Chandler. He was scouting and headed towards the next town on my schedule. It was 100 miles away and it seemed like 1,000. He chewed tobacco and he carried this little tin can. He'd chew, bring the can to his lips and spit. Chew, spit, chew, spit. After a while, the smell was sickening. He never seemed to notice, and it was right under his nose.

I've hired cabs for long hauls, Boise to Pocatello once. And I've had to hire a few charter planes too.

Once, I got stuck in Minneapolis. Somehow, I missed my connection. There was an airline strike and I'm pacing around the airport when this guy starts to talk to me. He had a son playing college hockey and he was on his way to see him play. Turns out the guy is president of Northwest Airlines. I tell him I've got to get to Minot, South Dakota. He makes some calls, gets me on a mail plane. I have to lie in the back, with the mail bags, but it got me there on time.

I've performed in Cuba, Canada, and Mexico. First time I was booked to play Chihuahua, start of a six-city tour, I forgot that you couldn't get into Mexico without proof of citizenship. I'm supposed to go from Juarez to Chihuahua, about 250 miles apart. I forget my passport. I try to fly from El Paso to Juarez and they won't let me get on without a passport. If I'd told them I was on vacation, I'd have had no problem. But I told them I was performing, and so they insisted I had to have a visa.

I get in touch with the American consulate. He writes out a proof of citizenship for me and issues a temporary passport. I get to Juarez, the plane has left. I'm going crazy. I find a cabdriver and I can't speak enough Spanish and he can't speak enough English. I'm going ba-ba-ba-baboom, making like I'm driving. Finally we find a guy who can interpret and we settle on $300 American money to drive to Chihuahua.

We drive through some of the most impoverished sights I've ever seen. And then, he gets a flat tire after 200 miles. The man has snow tires on his cab. It's 107 in the shade and he's got snow tires. He fixes the tire himself and we get to the town just before game time.

"Beisbol?" I'm screaming, trying to get directions to the ballpark. We get there, I rush in, get dressed, do my act—show went over great.

Nowadays, it's all plane travel. But there was a time when I tried driving from town to town. Bought myself a brand new DeSoto, so it had to be around 1953 or '54. I drive to Tennessee and now I've got to get from Johnson City to Lumberton, North Carolina. I'm going through Gastonia, coming down a hill, wham, some guy runs a stop sign and slams right into me. The car was totalled, but I was okay, except for some bumps and bruises.

I got to Lumberton somehow, did the show. But after

that I never took the car except to spots near Philadelphia, like Reading or Wilmington.

Stayed in a thousand lonely rooms, staring up at the ceiling where the fan ought to be, sweaty and tired, homesick, worried, thumbing through the train schedule, reading it by the dim light of a cracked lamp. I've stayed in hotel rooms so small, the mice were hunch-backed. I stayed in rooms so small, you had to step outside to change your mind.

Once I called the desk clerk and said, "I've got a leak in my room." and he said, "Okay, go ahead."

In the early days I'd stay in the same hotel as the visiting ballclub. You'd get there, you'd give the clerk 50 cents for a fan for your room. But if you weren't one of the first guys to register, you were out of luck.

And sometimes I'd get lucky. Once, in Eugene, Oregon I ran into Tommy Lasorda, who was managing Spokane. He said, "Hey, Max, don't check in, I've got a suite, you can room with me and save a few bucks." We get to the room, he says, "One thing, Max, if we lose the ballgame, I don't want to hear a word out of you. I'm a bad loser."

He looked serious when he said it. And I had seen him lose his cool—climb into the stands to get at hecklers.

It happens, he loses a tough ballgame. I get on the team bus to ride back to the hotel. He looks at me real hard and says, "Remember, Max, not one word out of you." We go get a bite to eat and he's stone silent. By now, it's an hour after the game, and I haven't spoken one word. We go back to the room and I'm dying. I don't think I've ever been that quiet that long. We're getting ready to go to sleep, he's about to turn the light out, when he says to me, "Max, what is it you want to tell me?"

I tell him to go spit in his hat. He had done the whole thing as a gag. He is a bad loser, though. That night, he had climbed into the stands again.

It's lonely on the road, and I've had my share of depressing moments.

Sometimes, your perspective gets jolted when a tragedy occurs. I remember doing a Fourth of July show in Butte, Montana. They set fireworks off on the side of a mountain just beyond the ballpark. After 10 minutes, the fireworks stopped suddenly. The fans grumbled, walked out of the ballpark saying it was the lousiest fireworks show they'd ever seen. What they didn't know, and what I didn't know until I picked up the paper the next morning, was that the guy operating the fireworks had had his head blown off.

Something hadn't ignited, he'd stuck his head into the tube to check it out, and the explosion blew his head off.

Another time I was doing a show in Des Moines and some kid had climbed a light tower because the place was sold out. He lost his grip, fell off and was killed.

I went through the motions, but I had no chance that night.

I know all about the corny notion that the show must go on. But some nights it's impossible. I was booked on a Saturday and Sunday in Chicago. That was the weekend Lyman Bostock got shot in Gary, Indiana, an innocent victim, riding in a car with the wrong person at the wrong time.

I come to the ballpark, Jim Fregosi is the Angels' manager, he's in the clubhouse, sad as can be. "Max," he said, "do whatever you want, I just don't give a damn."

Bostock was a fine player, a potential Hall of Famer. And now, he was gone. I called Bill Veeck and told him I wasn't going on. He said he wanted me to perform. I tried to explain it was no time for levity, that clubhouse was grim. But they had a good crowd, maybe 30,000 or so, and I got dressed in my uniform, figuring I'd go out there in the fourth inning.

I'm in the dugout, the phone rings, it's Veeck, saying, "Max, we've changed our mind, don't go on." It was Mrs. Veeck who changed his mind.

As sad as those guys looked, if you were a betting man, you'd have bet against the Angels that day. Well, the Angels won.

Chapter 7

NOTHING BUT THE TOOTH

I don't lug 20 bats to home plate any more. I don't somersault when I swing and miss. I still flop face first into bases, but I know I'm not as young as I used to be. I'm not even as tall as I used to be.

About eight years ago, I needed spinal surgery to remove a lower disc I had damaged through the years, flopping backwards as part of my act. Spent five hours on the operating table. This was three weeks before I was supposed to open my summer tour in Nashville. I told the doctor I was playing Nashville on June 1.

He said, "You can't do that. You've got to rehab the back for at least six weeks. You go out on the road, you're going against my wishes."

I went. I was scared to death, but I went. Still haven't missed a show in six decades. And that's despite prostate surgery, hemorrhoid surgery a couple of times, five or six broken fingers, hamstring pulls by the ton, broken toes, and the broken rib that came closest to breaking my streak of never missing a game.

I broke the rib in Wichita. Bucky Walters was managing that team. I staggered up there to hit, must have had 15 or 20 bats on my shoulder. The public address announcer says that Max Patkin will now show the Wichita Falcons how to hit. I stumble, intentionally. But this time one of the bats hits the ground barrel first and sticks like a spear. I fall onto it, and it breaks a rib.

The next day I'm booked in Denver. I'm in pain and I'm thinking about cancelling. Bob Howsam ran that club and had 23,000 in the stands at Mile High Stadium. He asked me to go on. Gene Mauch was in town with Minneapolis and he hated me. He blew his cork. He'd had me for three games that season and he'd lost every game. A pain in the ribs, coupled with a pain in the butt, but I went on, tip-toed through the act.

I got to Salt Lake City, the trainer from the University of Utah taped me up. I was hobbling for about three weeks, but I got through it.

Some of the injuries I've had down through the years were my fault. And some, I was simply an innocent victim.

Bob Uecker, who turned a mediocre big league career into fame and fortune as a comic, nearly shattered my streak in Louisville one night. Uecker had just struck out (something which he did many, many times.) Out of frustration, he took his hard, plastic batting helmet and he fired it towards the dugout. It skidded like a stone on a pond and wham! It hit the dugout wall right where I was sitting—caught me in the back of the head, opened a cut. I told him, "Just think, if it had hit me in the face, what it might have done to my looks."

I like to sit in the dugout for an inning or two before I go on, just to gather my thoughts, to get the feel of the game, a sense of the crowd. If you don't have your head in the game, you're liable to get it handed to you.

One night, in Toledo, Mike Epstein, who was playing first base for Rochester, smacked a line drive foul, right into the dugout. Nailed me on the shoulder. I carried that bruise for two weeks.

I wish I had a buck for every time I've been hit by a line drive while out there, coaching. I could retire. One time, I'm out there, my legs spread-eagled, my face close to the ground, and Willie Montanez hits a line drive right at my head.

I pull my neck in, the ball zips right past my nose close enough to count the stitches. I think that's the first time I ever saw Montanez laugh on the ballfield. Montanez was a flashy guy. The other players would say there wasn't enough mustard in the world to cover that hot dog.

And when I wasn't ducking line drives or skidding helmets, I had to be on the lookout for pranksters, guys messing with my props, getting a laugh at my expense.

In the old days, they had spittoons in the clubhouses. Guys smoked, chewed, spit. Well, Jimmy Dykes, who used to manage the A's, filled the water bucket prop with cigar butts and cigarette butts and all the yucky stuff from one of the spittoons. And then, when I pretended to faint from the smelly shoe, the trainer hustled out there and spilled all that garbage on me.

Another time, Walker Cooper was managing in Fort Worth, and he filled the bucket with beer. It was over 100 degrees that day, and now the trainer comes sprinting out there and pours the beer on me. I was wiping away suds for two innings.

Players have stuffed things like rubber snakes in my back pockets. When I reach in for the red hankies I use as signal flags, the snakes would come slithering out. Once it was a live toad, slimy and slick. Another time a dead mouse.

But all that is pretty tame compared to what they've done to my soda cans, the ones I use for "Old Faithful." Guys have taken the cans into the dugout latrine, emptied the cold water I ordinarily use, and then filled the cans with urine. Once, I went out there, gulped, realized it wasn't water, spit it out, and shouted to the dugout, "What is this, warm beer?"

The guys who weren't doubled up laughing, hollered, "No, you dumb so-and-so, that's piss." I've had guys pour vodka into the cans. And Frank Thomas once filled a can with Tabasco sauce. Couldn't pucker for a week.

People wonder how I'm able to spritz so many times on one long gulp of water. I tell them I keep the water in my mouth, but I pat my body and that confuses them.

It doesn't hurt that I only have that one crooked tooth in the front of my mouth. People are always asking me when my dentist retired. Actually, I decided to try a set of dentures when my upper teeth rotted and had to be removed. I went to this dentist in Northeast Philadelphia. I paid him $3,000 and he took impressions and got the teeth made. Now, I show up and he sticks the teeth in my mouth.

He ducks into the bathroom and I know he didn't have to go, because I never hear him flush the toilet. Instead I hear the sound of muffled laughter. Finally, he comes out and says, it just won't work, and he'll give me half my money back. I take the $1,500. He kept the teeth. They're probably in his drawer somewhere, smiling.

The single crooked tooth makes for some interesting dugout challenges. Players today love to chew on sunflower seeds during ballgames. They'll give me a handful and watch me struggle, trying to pry one open with that single crooked tooth. They'll bet me I can't eat five to their 25 and they win every time. Peanuts are even tougher, because the shells hurt my gums.

If I got distracted while I was getting dressed for my act, guys would rub Capsolin in my undershorts. Capsolin, that's hotter than liniment, hotter than Wintergreen, it's the stuff trainers rub on muscle aches.

You feel like your pants are on fire.

It created some wild dance steps, which got some laughs, so I chalked it up as the price you pay for laughter.

I can accept the practical jokes as part of the job. In Class A, the kids are seeing me for the first time, they're respectful. I perform in AA or AAA, the guys have seen me once, twice, maybe three times, they get a little frisky.

Most of the time, the gags are done with affection. It's the mean-spirited guys who trouble me, the guys who resent me being out there, the managers who won't let me dress in the clubhouse, who don't want me out there on the coaching lines during close games.

In the beginning, some of the hassles came out of misunderstanding over just what my act was all about. In the late 40's, Eddie Gottlieb booked me out of Philadelphia. We'd run an ad in *Sporting News* for about $75 (today, an ad that size would cost $600).

So Eddie books me into Cincinnati. Gabe Paul was the general manager. I get there, explain what I do, he goes nuts.

"What?" he screams. "Perform during the game? Nobody performs during a game."

He wasn't going to let me go on, unless I worked before the game. The Reds were playing the Phillies and I knew Robin Roberts and Maje McDonald and Granny Hamner. They see me dying out there because I didn't have a pre-game act.

I'm getting silence, with some scattered boos.

All of a sudden, four guys run out of the dugout. Robby, Maje, Hamner, and Puddin Head Jones. They start doing the shadow infield, where you pretend you're flipping a baseball around the diamond. Saved my act a little. After I finished, Gabe Paul said I was so bad he wasn't going to pay me. Two or three weeks later, he sent Gotty a check along with a note saying to forget about booking that guy again.

The first serious hassle came while I was still working for Bill Veeck in Cleveland. He'd send me out to minor league parks from time to time, and now, they book me in Buffalo, in 1947. I'm supposed to do the whole weekend, Friday, Saturday, Sunday and they've run big ads about Max Patkin, the coaching clown from Cleveland.

I get to the ballpark and Paul Richards is managing Buffalo. I tell him I'm going to coach, on the lines, for two or three innings. He raises hell. This was a guy from Waxahacie, Texas, a real purist. He refuses to let me go on. The general manager explains how they've spent money to advertise me, and Richards insists he wants me to do 20 minutes pre-game. Finally, he caves in.

Now, I've got to go see Billy Meyers, who is managing the Newark Bears, to get his permission. He says no. I talk him into it. Then I go see the umpires. They say no. Finally, they call Clark Shaughnessy, the president of the league. He says that as long as neither team is protesting, I can go on. Now, Meyers says that when I'm coaching for Newark, I have to change shirts, put on a Newark shirt. For three days I got booed, I got cheered—boo, cheer, boo, cheer.

Sometimes, I got the last laugh. Clay Bryant managed

Newport News, a Dodgers farm club. This was around '48 or '49. Bryant was a tough, hard-nosed manager, who disliked my act. I perform, they lose the game, and I'm in a corner of the clubhouse, peeling off my uniform. Bryant takes a chair and he's banging it against the wall out of frustration. He bangs it and bangs it and it won't break. Here's a guy, six-four, 200 pounds, and the damn chair wouldn't break.

Red Rolfe was another guy who hated my act. I understand. Deep down, I'm a purist too. But I try not to interfere with the flow of the game.

I'm out there, one day, coaching first, imitating the first baseman the way I still do. Walt Dropo was playing first, coming off an injury. He'd just gotten back in the lineup, we're in Detroit, and he whispers out of the side of his mouth, "Please, don't do it. If I help you and he knows it, he'll yank me out of the lineup."

After I worked with Veeck in St. Louis, with the Browns, I went out on my own, one-night stands, strictly minor league ballparks. My brother, Eddie, came with me. I needed a shoulder to lean on, someone to talk to, someone to tell me I was funny, and that I could make it as a baseball clown. You could have put my self-confidence in a thimble in those days and had room left over.

W.T. Anderson, who was president of the Georgia-Alabama League, refused to let me perform. George Trautman, head of the minor leagues, even sent out a directive that was supposed to be posted in every ballpark in the country. It said that no one was allowed to coach during a ballgame, that no one was to distract from the ballgame. I'd get to a town, they'd say they couldn't use me, I'd get on the bus and go on to the next town.

After a while, when I started getting good notices, Anderson wrote me a letter, saying I was welcome in the Georgia-Alabama League.

It's strange, but some of the guys who hate my act are friendly once the game is over. A guy like Bill Norman, for example. And other guys won't have anything to do with me, on or off the field. Harry and Dixie Walker, are like that—rednecks. I run into Harry at banquets and he won't even say "Hello." I think there's some bigotry involved there.

A guy like Eddie Stanky, from Philadelphia, he didn't like me performing. But he was a sensitive guy, inside. I remember when he left college coaching to come back to managing in the major leagues. He lasted one game. Walked out to the mound to talk to a pitcher, I think it was Bert Blyleven. And the pitcher said, "What the bleep are you doing out here?"

Stanky made a U-turn, went back to the dugout. After the game, he peeled off his uniform and left town.

Stanky, Mauch, Dick Williams, guys like that who wanted to squelch me, I could understand it. They were dedicated to the game, they accomplished something as players or managers. It was guys like Wally Moon that baffled me. Moon was managing in Frederick, Maryland, and the ballpark was sold out, standing room only. Moon told me he wasn't going to let me perform. I went to the general manager, who took Moon aside. The general manager came to me and said that Moon told him I'd been drunk once, while performing in San Antonio.

That was ridiculous. I never drink before a performance. I can barely eat, my stomach is so fluttery. There have been times when I've been invited to a pre-game cocktail party and I might sip at a drink to be sociable. But drunk? Never!

Of all the managers who tried to keep me out of their ballparks, Jim Bunning was probably the most persistent. Bunning is a Congressman now—kissed babies, shook hands, smiled all the time, when he ran for election. Somehow I have a hard time picturing that. At the ballpark he had a personality like sandpaper.

Bunning started out managing Reading. I have appeared in Reading 34 of the last 35 years. The year I missed? The year Bunning managed there. I got a call from Jim Bronson, the general manager. Told me he was going to have to cancel me that year, even though I had drawn standing room only crowds year after year. I wanted to know why and he said I'd have to talk to Bunning, who was on the road, in West Haven.

I got the number, called him, and said, "I understand you're the one who cancelled me out. Why?"

And he said, "Let me tell you something, Max, when I was pitching for Williamsport, maybe 20–25 years ago, I was getting beat that game and you were coaching first base, clowning around, I swore to myself that if I ever managed, I'd never let you in my ballpark."

Can you imagine a guy holding a grudge for so many years, and acting friendly to me the whole time?

A year later, I get a little revenge. Bunning is managing in Eugene. He finds out I'm booked there. I get a call from the general manager out there, and he says, "Max, Jim Bunning doesn't want you to perform. But I called up Dallas Green [who was head of the farm system for the Phillies then] and I told him, 'Max Patkin is gonna perform in my ballpark, and if Jim Bunning doesn't let him in my ballpark, I'm gonna take Bunning's clothes and toss 'em out in the street.'"

It was strange, because Bunning had pitched in Philadelphia, where Bill Giles was always thinking up stunts to please the fans. He had a hang-glider guy deliver the first ball one year. The guy called himself Kiteman and he crashed into the seats and the fans booed him. And Giles even had the chimp, J. Fred Muggs, sweep the bases once. And he even had the Great Wallenda walk a high wire across the stadium.

Bunning would have grumbled and said, well, those acts were performed *before* the game, not *during* the game.

The thing is, I had an ace in the hole. Paul Owens was the Phillies' general manager the year Bunning was in Eugene. Owens nearly got me killed one year, in Canada. Owens was playing first base for Olean and I'm behind him, imitating him. On the last throw, he's supposed to let the ball go by and I grab it. Well, he got mixed up on the signs and he missed a throw before I was ready. Whoosh, it went right by my ear. I wasn't expecting it, and if it had hit me, he would has busted my nose for sure.

Owens owed me one. But I didn't have to cash the marker. I show up, and Bunning has given orders that I can't dress in his clubhouse. I like to dress with the home team, go over my act, get to know them.

I coach first base, and then, he allows me to coach third, which I didn't think he would. It's a scoreless game, and I'm coaching in the third and fourth innings. Fourth inning, I'm coaching third, I spread-eagle my legs, peer in towards the catcher, make believe I'm stealing the signs. I walk down four or five feet and I holler, "Fast ball, fast ball" to the batter. And now, the pitcher throws a fast ball and the hitter knocks it out of the ballpark.

Eugene wins the game, 1–0. After the game, a photographer comes over, and asks Bunning if he'd pose with me. He posed.

The next year, I saw him at the New York baseball writers' dinner. We were in Ed Mosler's suite, having cocktails before the dinner. Bunning came over to me, and he said, "Max, you won't believe this, but I have that picture of you and me on my desk.

"Every once in a while I look at that picture and I say to myself, 'Please, Jim, don't take yourself so serious.'"

Bunning had a great career, a no-hitter in the American League, and a perfect game in the National League—even if it was against the Mets—won a lot of games, struck out a lot of guys. Maybe it was that attitude he had that has kept him out of the Hall of Fame?

Jim Palmer was that way too, surly, gloomy, very serious. Palmer was the starting pitcher in one of the craziest performances of my life. It happened in Toronto.

The Blue Jays were new in the league, far out of it, while Baltimore and the Yankees were fighting for the American League East pennant. Toronto wasn't playing its regulars against contending teams and there was a big stink about that. Peter Bavasi, the Toronto general manager, had booked me before the season started. And now, it was September, a Sunday afternoon, and all the American League brass is up there to check things out.

Lee McPhail, the league president was there. So was Dick Butler, in charge of the umpires, and my old friend Johnny Stevens, an umpire supervisor. They're telling Bavasi that the worst thing in the world would be to have a clown out there.

They ask Earl Weaver, who was managing Baltimore, how he felt and he said he'd worked with me as a player and a manager in Appleton, in Elmira, and in Rochester, and that I knew how to coach and wouldn't hurt anybody.

Butler wanted me out there in the first and second innings, coaching third. They had a television camera in the third base dugout and Stevens was going to be giving me orders, what I could do and what I couldn't do. If a runner got on base, they wanted me out of there. When I told the Toronto guys that, somebody yelled, "Don't worry Max, nobody is gonna get on base."

I go out there, I'm coaching third and I'm giving all sorts of signs. The batter steps out, exaggerates like he's paying attention. He winds up out of the batter's box for 30 seconds, and that's too long.

Stevens is screaming for me to get the guy back in the batter's box. First two guys make out. Now, John Mayberry is the hitter for Toronto. I pretend to steal the signs. Palmer throws him a lousy curve ball. I figure he's gonna come back with a fast ball, so I yell to Mayberry, "Hey, Mayberry, fast ball."

Palmer throws a fast ball, Mayberry hits it out of the ballpark. I high-five him as he comes around third, I'm strutting, the crowd is laughing. I glance over and Palmer is off the mound, steely-eyed, staring at me for maybe 15 seconds. If looks could kill, I'd have been dead right there.

The next inning I finish my act, get a big hand, it's still a 1–0 game. I get a call from Early Wynn, who was doing color on radio. He wanted to interview me on the air. So seventh inning, I go up there, it's still a 1–0 game and Palmer has a one-hitter. The press box is loaded because of the pennant race and guys tell me that if Toronto wins the game, 1–0, I'm the most valuable player.

Ninth inning, Eddie Murray hits a homer to tie the

game. Eleventh inning, Murray hits another homer, but Toronto ties it. Thirteenth inning, Murray hits another homer, but Toronto rallies, wins the game.

Palmer does a post-game interview and says, there's no way a clown should be working a game of this magnitude. He might have been right, because it was September, and there was a pennant race.

But another time, I brought some good luck to the Yankees. This was early in the season. George Steinbrenner had bought the Yankees and booked me. I get to Yankee Stadium and Ralph Houk, the Yankee manager, says, "Get out of my clubhouse, I'm trying to win a pennant."

It was May and he's yelling about winning a pennant. The Yankees had lost four or five in a row, and maybe that explains things? I told him it wasn't my idea, that Mr. Steinbrenner had hired me. Besides, I was booked for two weekends and I didn't want to blow the payday, or the chance to perform in Yankee Stadium. Finally, somebody persuaded Houk to rub my nose for luck.

He reached over like it was a snake and he rubbed it. Sure enough, the Yankees won that day. Won the next three games, too.

Three weeks later, I got a check. He paid me $150 a show. I couldn't believe it. I was losing that much every day, playing gin rummy. (A couple of years later, Steinbrenner gave Catfish Hunter $3 million a year to pitch.) Years later, I got a nice note from Steinbrenner. It said, "I follow you in press and now movies. Costner's a better actor but you definitely have the female appeal. See you soon."

Bob Scheffing, when he was general manager of the Mets, booked me for Shea Stadium, for that Mayor's Fund charity game where the Mets play the Yankees, but he was overruled by somebody in the front office.

Before the cancellation, Leonard Koppett wrote a column in the *Sporting News* predicting pennants for the Yankees and Mets, because the last time I had appeared in New York, in 1951, with the St. Louis Browns, the Yankees won the American League pennant and the Giants and Dodgers had tied for the National League flag. That was the only time in baseball history that three teams from one city all finished first. Bobby Thomson hit that famous homer to win the Giants-Dodgers playoff.

Scheffing didn't seem to care about history, or about the handshake we'd had. When I got to the ballpark, he said I could do my "Rock Around the Clock" dance and I could imitate the first baseman, but I couldn't stay out there on the coaching lines.

Actually, he didn't have the decency to tell me that. He sent Art Richman, the public relations guy, to tell me the bad news. As it turned out, the Yankees were kicking the hell out of the Mets, something like 10–1 that day and commissioner, Bowie Kuhn, called me over and said, "Max, why don't you go out and coach?"

I told him I'd been squelched. He said I should to tell the manager that, as a favor to him, he'd like me to perform. I was uncomfortable doing it, but I tried, and the manager refused.

I was really crushed.

I do remember that 1951 visit vividly, though. The Yankees had Vic Raschi and Allie Reynolds pitching in a doubleheader. The Brown were in last place. On merit.

We won the opener. And then we got a couple of runs off Reynolds early. I was out there, working the coaching line, and we got four or five more runs.

Mike Burke, the chief executive officer of the Yankees, stood up in the pressbox and said, "I wish I had a shotgun... I'd shoot that son-of-a-bitch!"

Chapter 8

ODDS AND ENDS

There was a time when I could be sitting in a bar, with a bunch of guys, and I'd make a bet on who would come in the door next, a blonde or a brunette?

That's sick.

It's one thing to gamble, to take your chances. It's another thing to gamble when the deck is stacked against you. That's sicker.

I'd go to the fights, the guy next to me would always sucker me into betting the red corner all night long. Years later I discover that they always put the champion or the heavy favorite in the blue corner.

I don't know when it started or why it started. I looked around, I wasn't any different than the other kids growing up in the neighborhood. We'd flip baseball cards, winner take all. (If I had kept all those baseball cards, they'd be worth a fortune today.) We'd pitch pennies, tossing them to the wall. Closest to the wall wins. We had no money then, so the stakes were pennies or baseball cards or the hazel nuts we'd shoot (we were city kids, we didn't have marbles). You put the nut between your thumb and your index finger and you flicked it towards the target nut. Winner keeps all the nuts out there.

I didn't start to gamble for money until I had some money. I played a little pinochle, small stakes. I started playing golf—became a decent player. Best I ever got was a 10 handicap.

It wasn't long before I was playing $25 Nassaus. That's $25 on the front nine, $25 on the back nine, and $25 for the match—plus automatic presses.

I lost so much money I had to borrow from my brother Eddie. I was playing with guys of the same caliber, but they had more money, so there was no pressure on them to sink a putt worth $100. Lee Trevino says pressure is playing a $5 Nassau with $2 in your pocket. He's right. If you're scared, your knees shake, and that four-foot putt looks like it's 40 feet.

It got so bad I couldn't sink a putt the size of my nose.

We'd play poker at least once a week. It started out a quarter, fifty cents, a dollar ,and it went up from there. Pretty soon I was playing cards every night of the week. I borrowed from my brother, from banks.

By 1951 I had saved about $50,000 from ballpark appearances, from dance exhibitions, from sports shows. Over the next 10 years that all went down the toilet.

I got so desperate I'd ask for advances on my appearances. I was only making $250 a game then, with a rainout guarantee of $35 or $50. I'd ask for a deposit.

I was single, I was living the life of a playboy eight months of the year. There were 57 minor leagues in those days, so I had plenty of work during the summer months. I'd be on the road from May until August, hustling from town to town, depending on the trains and buses to get me there. They'd leave the train windows open in those days, and I'd get to the next town covered with soot.

The rest of the year I'd sleep late, head for the Philadelphia Athletic Club on Broad Street, play some basketball, nap, hit the steam room, and then get dressed and go out night-clubbing until four in the morning.

If I got lucky, fine. If not, I'd go home to sleep, alone. Next day, same routine.

I never played the numbers. I think the lottery is a joke. It's like a tax on poor people to supposedly help old people. That's a sucker's bet, 500-to-1 on the daily number when it ought to be 999-to-1.

Sure, I'd give the doorman at the 2-4 Club a buck every now and then to play 627 for me, just to give him some action. I knew every big numbers writer in town. I'd hang out in the after-hours joints and I'd see them there. I just liked the atmosphere. Some days I'd play golf at Iron Rock with Cozy Morley, who is still doing nightclub comedy; a guy named Skinny Razor, who was a hit man for the mob; and Felix Bocchicio, who managed Sonny Liston for a while. We'd play $100 a hole. My game improved, but my luck didn't. One day I lost $1,500. It was no fun after a while. Every shot was for big money. I'd look around, I'd see guys cheating, kicking the ball out of the woods, that kind of thing.

I never bet on baseball or basketball. I played those parlay cards in football, where you have to pick four teams against the point spread. I had enough trouble picking one winner, what chance did I have to pick four?

I went out to Las Vegas and blew $1,500 on one trip. That's equivalent to $10,000 today. Lost most of it playing blackjack.

Once, during the summer, I flew from Pocatello to Las Vegas because I had an open date. Some show girl latched onto me. I was slipping her $50 or $100 every time I won a hand.

Pretty soon, she invited me to her house. I only had a couple of hundred bucks left by then. We get there, she says we'll play strip poker. I'm trying like crazy to lose all my clothes, and I get down to my jockey shorts when... boom, her father walks in. End of game.

I never got caught up in betting horses. Went to watch the trotters a few times. I remember the first time I ever went to Liberty Bell Racetrack in Northeast Philly. It's a shopping mall now.

First race ended, I started waving a ticket, hollering, "I've got the winner, I've got the winner."

Second race, same thing. "I've got the winner," I'm yelling.

Third race, people were asking me for advice. They're coming from all over to ask me who I liked in the race. I didn't have the heart to tell them I was betting on every horse in the race. I wound up losing $40 for the night, but I had a few laughs.

When we couldn't get a poker game together, I'd play gin rummy, because you only needed two guys for that. Played for a penny a point in the beginning. It adds up. I guess the worst episode was playing gin rummy with Dizzy Dean on a flight into Philadelphia. We start out playing a penny a point and I'm down $70, so we up it to two cents a point. The rule was: once the wheels touched down, if the game wasn't complete, it didn't count.

Well, he's got me blitzed in the first two games as we're coming in for the landing. Blitzed means blanked, shut out, and that doubles the damage. I'm delaying, stalling. Finally I throw a card. Delay some more, throw another card. Third card, bango, he hollers, "Gin!"

I pick up the deck of cards and I heave them, all over the plane. Pretty soon, here comes the stewardess with most of the cards.

She leans in, says sweetly, "Are these your cards, sir?"

I tell her, "Yeah, they're mine, and you can take 'em and stick 'em up your keister."

Looking back, I'm ashamed. But that's what gambling does to you.

My brother finally straightened me out. Took charge of my finances, put me on a budget. I haven't done any serious gambling since I got divorced.

Occasionally I might make a small wager on an Eagles' game just to have a rooting interest. And I'll play gin rummy at the health club for a quarter of a cent a point. And I play with guys worth a ton of money, but it isn't about money, it's about ego. At the end of the game, a guy who owns Paintarama will take out a roll of bills that would choke a horse and he'll peel off $6 to settle up. If I lose $16, that's a big day. It took me a lot of years, a potful of money to realize I'm not that good a player.

I'm frugal now. A big night is taking my daughter and her husband out to dinner. I go dancing at least once a week, but they know I'm going to put on a show so they skip the admission charge.

I don't miss the gambling. It's a sickness and I'm better off without it.

Chapter 9

WEDDING DAY BLUES

When you grow up gawky, and your nickname is "Big Nose" you are not going to have a lot of girlfriends. You can count your sexual experiences on the fingers of one hand—if you know what I mean.

My first brush with sex came with a next door neighbor who lived on Rodman Street. I used to watch her get undressed, peeping through my window, across the alley to her house. She was around 19, easy. Everybody in the neighborhood boasted about having her. Everybody but me.

And then one day she asked me if I wanted to take a walk with her?

I started stuttering. S-s-s-s-sure, I finally said.

We started walking, towards 63rd street, that's where Cobb's Creek Park is. People used to promenade there on weekends. We stop, I start groping her. She says we'll go behind a hedge and we'll do it. I stutter even more.

And just then, a car drives by, some guy yells, "Hey, baby, wanna go for a ride?"

Bingo, she takes off.

I was scared to death of women. It wasn't until I got to be a good dancer that anybody paid any attention to me. Women liked to dance, and they knew I'd put on a show and people would notice them, too.

My first real sexual experience—though I guess this one doesn't count either—came in a house of ill repute in Chester. It was right across the street from the Ford plant, so it did plenty of business.

The women would parade around in bathing suits. You picked one, you paid a dollar, and you went upstairs. Me, I was 16 and I was scared to death—scared I wouldn't do it right, scared the joint would be raided and I'd be kicked off the baseball team.

I brought a rubber, took forever to get it on. And then I was so scared, nothing really happened. She kept the buck anyway.

There were some romances down the line. Some heartache too. A woman in St. Louis who claimed I was the father of her baby hit me with a paternity suit. It wasn't mine, but Bill Veeck, who owned the Browns then, paid her off and she stopped bugging me.

I had my share of one-night stands, but mostly, especially after a ballgame, I'd dance 'em, and the players would romance 'em.

I had one love affair with a girl who sold magazines in Philadelphia. That didn't work out. She called me recently. She's living in Long Branch, said she'd like to see me. I lied. I told her I was going steady.

Maybe that bit of background will help you understand why I married a beautiful woman, 17 years younger than me, and why our marriage turned into a nightmare that finally ended after she tried to bust open my skull with a hammer.

She was 17 when I met her. Her name was Judy Oberndorf and she was beautiful—a tall blonde with big bazooms. She was working as a cigarette girl in a center city nightclub, depending on tips. (Cigarette girl, that means she sold cigarettes. The old George Raft movies, girl in a skimpy costume comes around, with a tray and says, "Cigars? Cigarettes?")

When I met her, she worked in the Embassy Club, downtown. All the big league players hung out there. (Good food, a gathering place for characters, stayed open late, Sam Silver owned it, kept a huge mastiff out in front of the door.) Her father had tossed her out of the house and she was living with a girlfriend on Spruce Street, two blocks away from the nightclub.

I went with her for seven years, seeing her once or twice a week. I wasn't making a lot of money in those days, maybe $125 or $150 a game, depending on the size of the ballpark. I wasn't talking marriage. Eventually, her father took her back, into the house. I'd go out to pick her up for a date, or she'd meet me in town.

After seven years of this, her mother confronted me one night, in the kitchen. Basically, she said I had to shit or get off the pot. She said I was wasting her daughter's time, and I ought to marry her or disappear.

I decided to ask her to marry me. I was trembling. I could barely get the words out. I finally said, "W-w-w-w-w-we'll get married." And, as soon as I said it, I couldn't believe I'd said it. The next day I said goodbye to my father and I headed for California. I got as far as Baltimore.

I hid at the Lord Baltimore Hotel for two solid days, brooding, thinking about what I had done. My family was worried sick, wondering what had become of me.

Judge Leo Weinrot had always told me that any day, any time of day, he'd marry me. I called his secretary, made an appointment. That morning, I cut myself 30 times trying to shave. I can't even remember who my best man was. Judge Weinrot opened his office. Maybe two or three people were there. He needed witnesses, I think he took two handymen off the street.

We got married twice, actually. We had a rabbi marry us at Keneth-Isreal, a big synagogue. Then we headed for our honeymoon at the Sheraton Hotel, downtown. I thought I'd be romantic and carry her over the threshhold, but she was a big girl, and I couldn't lift her—I botched it.

I wasn't happy, yet I was happy. I was in shock, mostly.

I'm not sure why she married me. I was well-known, well-liked. Maybe she simply liked someone who was different. And I *was* different. She acted like she was in love with me.

Me, I'd always been intrigued by beauty. Maybe because I was so homely. I've always felt good about walking into a place with a gorgeous woman by my side.

I'd already accepted a job in Chicago with the ice show. I told her she could come out to Chicago once a month. I was there for almost seven months. She'd come out for a week at a time.

When I came back, we moved in with her folks. Big mistake.

Her father would see me in the morning, ask me what I was gonna do that day. I'd say, "Play golf." Then he'd ask me what I was gonna do tomorrow? And I'd say, "Play golf."

I'd sleep late... I was used to a certain way of life in the off-season. He tried to be nice to me, took me to the Meadowlands, a terrific country club, picked up the tabs. He was a lousy golfer.

Then we moved out, lived in the Presidential Apartments for a while, and things seemed to be going along okay.And then we bought a house—in the suburbs! She was compuslive about cleanliness. She'd get up at six in the morning and start cleaning the house.

After a while, she got very demanding. One year I had to buy her a full-length, white mink coat... I bought her a car...

And then the cheating started.

I'd go to the Philadelphia Athletic Club, work out, use the sauna. And I'd get phone calls. The guy would say, "It's your wife."

She'd tell me to bring home such-and-such, and the guys would say, "Your wife must love you, as often as she calls you."

Hey, she knew it was a 45-minute drive from the Athletic Club to our house. She'd make sure I was still there, and she'd invite some guy over. Years later, I found her little black book.

The list included some of my *best* friends.

She started drinking. She got hooked on Percodan. I didn't know anything about drugs. I didn't know how addictive Percodan was. I didn't know what a dangerous thing it was to do, mix alcohol and Percodan.

Then one day, my wife said we'd have to get separate bedrooms. She said I snored too much. I didn't think I snored that much. She played a tape recording for me, said she'd taped me snoring. Sounded like two lions in the zoo. I believe her and move into another bedroom.

She was so demanding. I look back, wonder why I put up with so much crap.We had a quarter acre of ground out in back of the house. She wanted a pool. I had to appease her, I got a pool built.

Once, I was in Honolulu. I called her, said I'd be home around four the next afternoon. I caught a red-eye flight out of Hawaii, flew to Los Angeles, flew out of L.A. to Philly, I got in at 4:30, she's sitting by the pool with a bunch of people, having a good time. Here, I'd been away, on a tough trip, and the first thing she says is, "Max, the lawn hasn't been cut."

Like a schmuck, I get the lawnmower, cut the lawn.

And though she might have been a good hostess with her friends, she wasn't with me. Once I was sitting out back, I was thirsty, I asked her to bring me a screwdriver. She comes out, five minutes later, with a real screwdriver. Another time, I bought a half-pound of corned beef, some cole slaw, some kaiser rolls. I ask her for two sandwiches, one with cole slaw, one without. She brings out one corned beef sandwich, one cole slaw sandwich.

I dated her for seven years and we were married for 10 years and in all that time, she never went to see me perform once. I tell people now, maybe she thought I was an airline pilot.

I guess the craziest thing we did together was the funeral for my dog. She loved that dog more than she loved me. He had cancer and we had to put him to sleep. I held the dog while the vet gave him the needle. That was hard to do. Then she decides she wants to have a funeral for the dog. They put him in a special box. There's a pet cemetery in Horsham. We go to the chapel, they play music, sad songs, take the coffin out, bury the dog, a guy reads a sermon at the grave site, saying what a nice dog he'd been—cost me a couple of hundred bucks, which was a lot more than I paid for the dog. He was a mongrel, got him from the ASPCA.

After a while, she said she wanted a baby. We tried to have one, but my sperm count was low. Her friends had kids, she wanted a kid. So we decide to adopt.

At first, I didn't want to do it. I knew I'd be away most summers and I wasn't sure what kind of mother she'd be. But a good friend of mine was a doctor and he knew about this baby girl who'd just been born, whose parents had been killed in an auto wreck. He arranged it, and we drove up to Presbyterian Hospital. He came outside, carrying the baby, and handed her to us.

We named her Joy, after her mother. Joy Sharon, the Sharon as a tribute to my father, Sam. We adopted her on May 20, 1963.

Right after that, I had to leave on my minor league tour. The baby was colicky, a difficult child. And it wasn't long before my wife's nerves were shot. She had a terrible temper and not much patience. She'd spank Joy, scold her, tell me what a burden she was.

In those days, I'd book 10 or 12 day trips and Joy got bitter, me being away so long. I tried to make up for it while I was home. I'd take her for walks in the park. I'd take her to the zoo. I used to say I needed to buy two tickets. One to get in and one to get out. I took her to the circus, to ballgames. She loved to pick flowers. When we moved to the house in Roslyn, she was always walking around, snatching flowers. The neighbors hated that.

Joy went through some tough times. Kids can be cruel and her classmates knew about the parade of men going in and out of our house while I was on the road and they teased her about it.

She'd have some fights, but after a while, she just shrugged it off. She went through some bad stages, as most kids do. Hung around with the wrong crowd. But basically, she turned out terrific, and she's happily married now. It takes a resilient kid to go through what she went through. Her attitude now is, hey, stuff happens, you go on.

She remembers my birthday, she never forgets me on Father's Day, we get along fine. Me, I'll never forget how she saved my life.

As a U. S. Navy enlistee, I went from a skinny sailor to a chief specialist, 1942–1944.

The Wisconsin State Rapids, 1941, with me, the flame-throwing right-hander, Max Patkin, in the top row, third from left.

The Base 8 Hospital Crew, Hawaii, 1945. I'm in the back row, at the far left.

The Indians visited a Universal Studio set and we met actress Ella Raines, 1947.

Me, all dressed up
in top hat and tails
for a dance routine
in Cincinnati,
performing with
Connie Boswell.

A rare, serious moment as Cleveland coach, 1946.

Here I am mugging with Bob Nieman, who hit back-to-back homers in his first major-league game, 1951.

Here, I'm alerting the hitter to look for the low pitch, League Park, Cleveland, 1946.

Here I am demonstrating the proper grip on a knuckleball while with the Browns.

Me, answering a heckler in a suave fashion.

Me, with a load of lumber—18, count 'em, 18 bats.

Here I am demonstrating my pitching and batting form.

Fielding form that drove my coaches crazy.

How to hit the ankle-high curve ball.

Me, driving them batty!

Bases loaded,
Mickey Mantle up,
who's scared?

Sam, you made the pants too long.

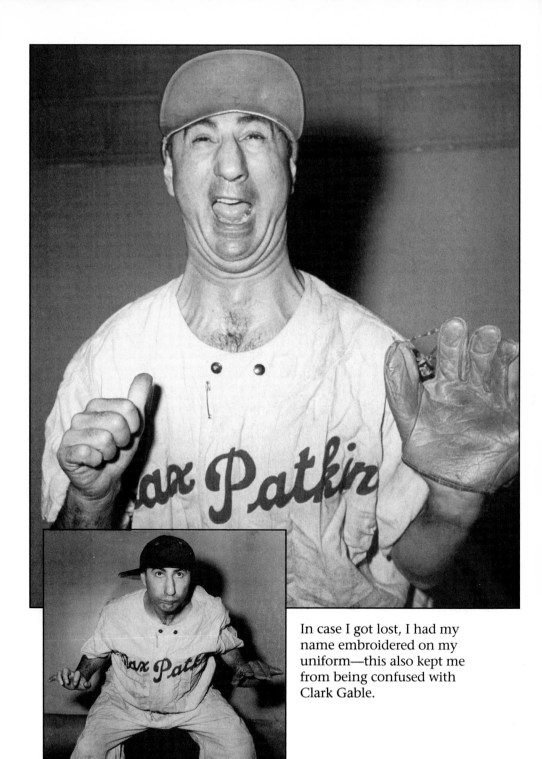

In case I got lost, I had my name embroidered on my uniform—this also kept me from being confused with Clark Gable.

Always the coach, here I am demonstrating proper jitterbug form at Fenway park (above) and fielding posture (right).

I finally found someone I could strike out after an ice show appearance at Chicago's Hilton Hotel.

They don't make belts like they used to…

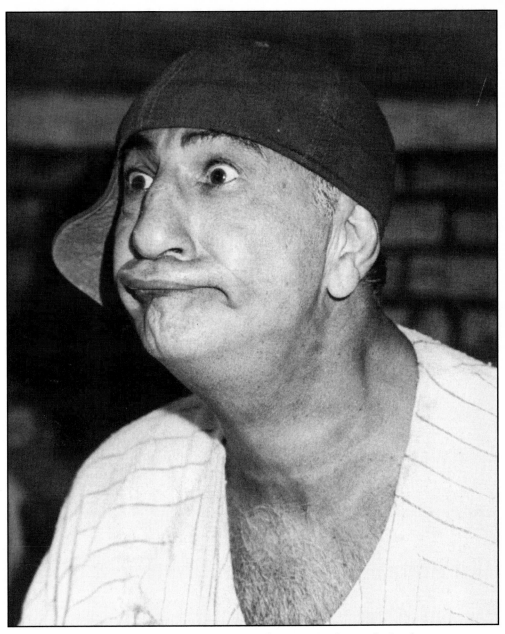

Here I am showing off the revolutionary sideways cap I popularized.

That's no chip on *my* shoulder when I go to bat!

Here I am signing autographs for some young fans. I'm still covered in shaving foam from the act. *Credit: Janet Kelly*

A handshake for a honey in Harrisburg. *Credit: Janet Kelly*

Oh say can you see... me standing for the national anthem. *Credit: Dave Kraus*

One more one-
night stand
over with.
*Credit:
Dave Kraus*

This is me performing at the Dream Game reunion of the 1962 Dodgers and Giants in Phoenix.

One of my classic poses—dirty and disheveled, in Cedar Rapids, Iowa.

When the Mets were lovable losers, I wore this uniform.

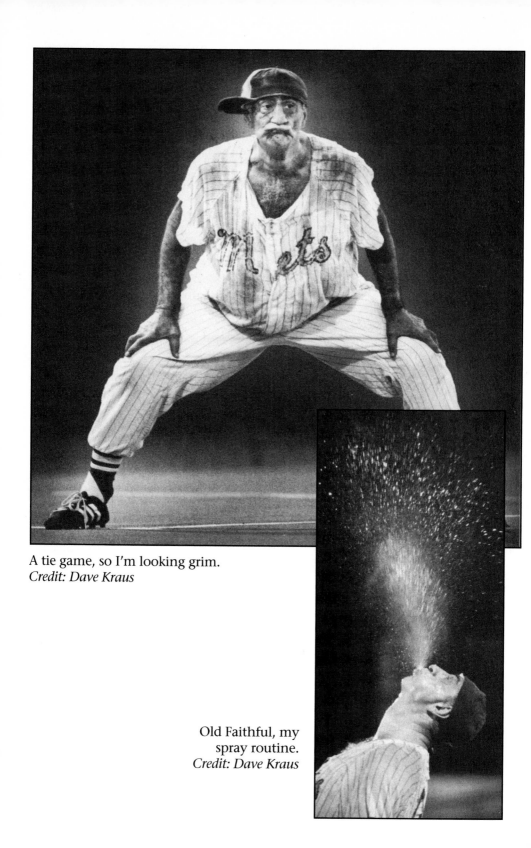

A tie game, so I'm looking grim.
Credit: Dave Kraus

Old Faithful, my
spray routine.
Credit: Dave Kraus

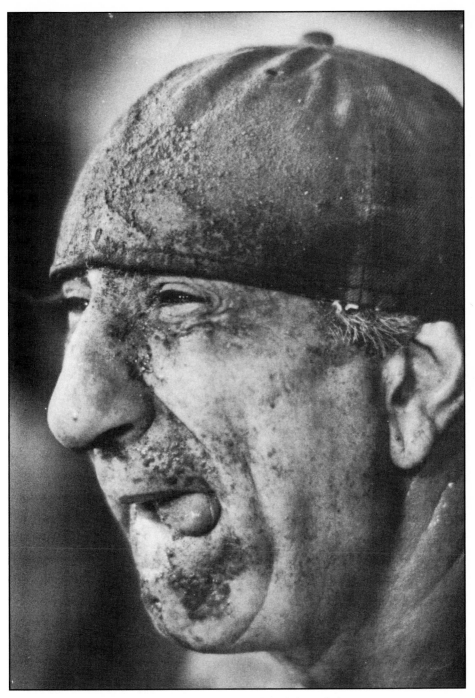

True Grit! Me, after one of my trademark head-first slides.
Credit: Dave Kraus

Hooray for Hollywood! My brother Eddie, Susan Sarandon, Kevin Costner, Ron Shelton, and the star of *Bull Durham*—me. *Credit: Paul Schumach*

Here I am posing with Orlando Cepeda, Juan Marichal, and Willie McCovey in Phoenix, 1987.

By George, he did it! Vice-President George Bush got some batting tips from me in Phoenix, 1987.

Olympic great Jim Thorpe appeared with me at Sportsman Shows in 1952 and gave me the undersized glove I use in my act to this day.

Say hey! It's me with Willie Mays at a charity golf tournament in 1992.

Here I am sharing a laugh with Los Angeles manager Tommy Lasorda at a banquet.

Me, Vic Lapiner, senior vice-president of Sales Boosters, and all-time hit leader Pete Rose at a golf tournament.

MAX PATKIN

THE CLOWN PRINCE

My very own
baseball card,
produced by
Procards, Inc.

MAX PATKIN
"The Clown Prince of Baseball"
HT: 6'3" **WT:** 185 lbs. **BORN:** Philadelphia, PA

Even though Max Patkin's name has never appeared in a major league box score, he is one of the best-known figures in baseball.

Since 1946 Patkin has made thousands of appearances in major and minor league ball parks as the "clown prince of baseball."

Max spent a year in the class D Wisconsin State League at Wisconsin Rapids in 1941, then joined the Navy after being released, spending most of his service time at Pearl Harbor.

After pitching briefly for Wilkes-Barre in 1946, Max was hired to do a comedy bit during an exhibition game between Harrisburg (Pa.) and the Cleveland Indians, whose manager, Lou Boudreau, recommended that he be hired as a major league coach.

After stints with the Indians in 1946-47 and the St. Louis Browns in 1951, Patkin went out on his own.

Now he travels 150,000 miles a year to fill the 90-100 engagements he makes during each baseball season.

"My one aim is to brighten the dull moments," says Max. "Even the umpires go along with my gags, as long as I don't foul up the game."

"But then, I work under a great handicap — I have no talent."

Printed courtesy of
PROCARDS, INC.

Bill Veeck, who gave me my start as a big-league clown, watching me in action at Comiskey Park. *Credit: Bill Miller*

Chapter 10

A Painful Split

I knew my marriage was coming apart at the seams even before my wife hired that teenaged handyman. He was about 17. Weekends, said she wanted to go to New Hope to look for antiques, and that she wanted to take the handyman with her. I'd sit there, at night, crying, waiting for her to come home.

She said she wanted more freedom.

She started staying out until three in the morning. And she'd never tell me where she'd been. She said she was going to leave me. I humbled myself, cried, begged her, asked her what I'd done wrong? She just said she needed her freedom. Even the guy who was supplying her with pain-killers and other stuff sat there in the kitchen one night and told me I ought to give her more freedom.

At one point, she said I ought to stay away for a few days. I went to see my lawyer. He told me to go home that night. So I did. Walked in, went upstairs, her bedroom door was closed. I opened the door and there she was, in bed with the handyman, this 17-year-old kid. I felt like someone had stuck a knife into my heart.

I started screaming at the kid and he jumps out of bed. He's stark naked and I'm chasing him around the house, through the kitchen, into the basement garage. I had a new set of golf clubs there. I also had a brand new freezer. I take out a six iron. He's hiding behind the freezer. I'm ready to swing at the guy and then I think, if I miss, I'm going to bust up that brand new freezer.

Now, when I tell the story, I say I missed him purposely, two swings, then two more, then two more. I tell people I bogeyed that hole, took a six.

She had been hanging out with hoodlums, gangsters,

drug dealers. I thought I'd better go out and buy a gun. I've still got it. At night, I'd lock myself in my room, with the gun under my pillow. Finally, I told her I didn't want that stream of bums coming in and out of my house. She said she wanted me out of the house.

One morning, she came home around six in the morning. Just after daybreak. I came downstairs. She seemed high as a kite. I turned my back on her and all of sudden, I'm being hit in the head with a hammer. My skull was split, blood was pouring out of the gash. As I fell, I fell against an expensive glass coffee table. Busted it into pieces.

She went to hit me again but the hammer handle was so bloodied, it slipped out of her hand.

She ran into the kitchen to get a knife and started after me again. Then my daughter jumped in, grabbed the knife, wrestled it away from her. I staggered out onto the lawn. My next door neighbor, who was an FBI agent, called the police. They came, took me to Abington Hospital. I was there for five or six days. When they discharged me, my head was still wrapped in bandages.

I was committed to attending a testimonial banquet for Tommy Lasorda in Norristown. Huge crowd, double dais. Mickey Vernon was there, Bobby Shantz. Joe Garagiola was the master of ceremonies. He's going down the line, introducing people, and he says, "There's Max Patkin, the Clown Prince of Baseball, he just got out of the hospital, his wife busted his head open with a ballpeen hammer."

Everybody laughed. They figured it had to be a joke. Some joke!

Obviously, it was time for a divorce. She wanted everything. She wouldn't talk about splitting property. She wanted it all, the house, the car, everything. What I wanted most of all was custody of our daughter. So I gave in on almost everything else, just so I could have Joy. After the divorce was granted, we moved in with my brother in his appartment in Huntington Valley.

She wound up marrying that kid, who was 18 years

younger than her—divorced him later on, married someone else. She had a couple of facelifts, moved to Arizona with the new husband.

And then, on her 50th birthday, she committed suicide. She simply couldn't stand getting old, I guess.

I went to the funeral, in Willow Grove, out of respect for my daughter. My father-in-law was sitting up front with his second wife and some close friends of his. There was a delay because the minister was late getting there.

He turned, said, "Why do we have to sit here so long?"

This was his only child. He'd treated her like garbage all those years and now he couldn't sit still for a few minutes. After his wife died, he remarried, and when he died, he left her every cent—didn't leave his only granddaughter a quarter. He might have been the most selfish man I've ever met.

The nightmare marriage took its toll. There I was, trying to be funny with a broken heart. One summer, I was booked in Mexico and I almost had a nervous breakdown. I had to play six cities in six days. I was laying on the trainer's table, shaking, burned out, ready to quit the tour.

I never smoked, which is one way some people calm their nerves. I was never any kind of drinker. I'd mix booze with ginger ale, never drink it straight. Bobby Maduro, the man who owned the Havana Sugar Kings, was there. He'd had a problem with depression, he had some medication. I think it was Valium. He urged me to try it. I didn't believe in drugs, but I couldn't eat, I couldn't sleep, I had to do something.

My brother Eddie got me through the worst times. He came on the road with me. I was so unsure of myself. I needed somebody in the room after a performance to pat me on the back, to tell me I'd been funny. Now, he's seen me so many times, he says there's no way I can make him laugh. He's probably right. But I needed somebody. The days would drag. I hate soap operas because they're so depressing. When you've got so much *tsoris* (sadness) in your own life, you don't want to watch a bunch of strangers involved in adultery, divorce, disappearances every afternoon.

It's hard to be funny when you're not eating, not sleeping, when you're so lonely. I was always on edge, every time I went out to the ballpark.

Even today, after 50 years of doing this corny act, I sit there, in the dugout before I go out, in a kind of trance. Ballplayers have said to me, "Max, you look like you're dead."

I'm trying to relax, cleanse my mind, forget my troubles. I go out there, I hear the laughter, I become a different person. Some guys play golf to forget their problems. Me, I get out on a ballfield, the crowd is with me, it's a whole different world.

Chapter 11

BLUE MOON AND EMPTY BALLPARKS

They've abandoned Durham Athletic Park. Built a new ballpark across town. I loved that old ballpark—not just because it was featured in the movie *Bull Durham*, but because the stands were close to the field, because the fans cared about the players, cared about the game, and because I could get a reaction, get some laughs, trade wisecracks with the old-timers.

In Durham, you'd get a blue collar audience. There'd be people there in overalls and you could smell the tobacco in the air... that's the best audience.

I have a tough time in the big new ballparks, with all that space behind home plate. All those foul balls get caught. I need foul balls rattling around in the stands. That way the pitcher has to rub up a new baseball, I get time to do my thing, get into a rhythm. That's why I like the ballparks in Reading, in Eugene, in Ashville. Spartanburg, that's another favorite of mine.

I've played Yankee Stadium and I've played Lowville, New York. And I've played every size in between.

Lowville, that's near Watertown, upstate New York. Did two days there in '52 or '53. County fair. I appeared with the town team. Half the guys were dressed in uniform, half weren't. The pitcher was out there, cigarette in his mouth. He gets set to pitch, puts the cigarette down on the back of the mound, and if that wasn't bad enough, they've got trotters and pacers racing around a dirt track around the field. The grownups are betting on the races. Only the kids were watching the ballgames. I couldn't wait to get out of that town.

Memphis was one of my first bookings. They assumed I was a pre-game act. I got there; they weren't going to let me perform. I had to talk Jack Onslow into it. Turned out to be one of the worst shows I ever did. Memphis scored four runs while I'm out there. Then Nashville scored five. I was booed so much, the manager finally said, "Don't go out there the next inning."

I came to love Memphis, except for this one appearance. I go up to bat, last part of my act, and the pitcher is losing the ballgame. He's pissed, and throws the ball at my feet—hits me in the foot! I tell him to stick the ball where the sun don't shine. The manager, Johnny Antonelli had to step between us. People are jeering, yelling. Later, when the kid got to triple-A, he came up to me, apologized. He said he was keyed up and he lost control.

Sometimes, big-time superstars come up to me and tell me about the first time they ever saw me perform. Reggie Jackson always remembered seeing me in Lewiston. Mickey Mantle knew it was somewhere in Oklahoma. And Willie Stargell, one of the nicest guys who ever played the game, said he first saw me in Roswell, New Mexico.

Stargell took his share of abuse in Roswell. Once a guy said he was bringing a shotgun to the park and was going to nail Willie. He played anyway. That was before he was known as "Pops."

I've had my share of trouble at some ballparks—a lot of it my fault. There was that one brutally cold day in Lethbridge, Canada, where I lost control, and I regret it. It was bitterly cold and it had started to snow. They shouldn't have been playing the game, and hardly anyone was in the stands. So I dropped my pants and mooned the crowd. Jim Lefebvre was the manager. I forget who the general manager was, but I got a letter from the club owner, squawking. He was right. I shouldn't have done it.

I'd say that 95 percent of my act is good, clean fun. The other 10 percent is a little raunchy, a little crude. Hey, math was never my best subject.

Sometimes, I'm not very discrete either. Like the time

at the major league meetings. I walk into Convention Center, and they've got all kinds of displays there. I grab a Little League bat and I put it between my legs.

I say, "How would you like to be built like this?"

Turns out, Mrs. Falwell is right behind me. Her husband owned the Lynchburg team. He was a first cousin to Jerry Falwell, the preacher. I get down on my knees, I plead with her, "Please, Mrs. Falwell, don't tell Mr. Falwell, or he'll excommunicate me."

She just smiles. I get up, walk away. Half-hour later, I'm telling the story in the lobby to some guys. I look around, there she is.

There was one game where I did wonder if I'd get out of the ballpark alive. It was in '67, and Chicago was gripped with racial tension. I'm playing Comiskey Park, a big game between the Indianapolis Clowns and the Kansas City Monarchs.

I'm the only white man on the field.

I'm warming up, and I'm making faces at the fans in the first base box seats. This guy throws beer at me. He thought I was being racist. I look around and think, I can get killed here. But I go out there, do my act. I finish, the guy who threw the beer calls me over, apologizes, said he didn't know what I was up to at first.

In the early days, it was exciting, going to new places, wondering what the crowds would be like. It was bad for my stomach and I couldn't sleep the night before, but it kept the juices flowing.

Bobby Maduro owned the Havana Sugar Kings when I first went to Cuba. Buffalo was leading the league and the game drew 25,000 people. The Sugar Kings were in last place. This was all new to me. I'm having trouble communicating. And now, Havana falls behind 4–0 early. I go out to coach in the fourth inning, and by that time, we're losing, 6–0. I move over to third base the next inning, and bingo, Havana scores 11 runs while I'm coaching third. I windmill the runners home, the crowd is going crazy.

I'm working the next day, the Sunday game. In the morning, I weigh myself. I'd lost 10 pounds on Saturday.

Sunday, Havana wins again. He books me back for the next year.

The next year, the plane is coming in for the landing, everybody's staring out the window. They've got a big red carpet rolled out. We're all looking around, to see who's important that's on the plane? Movie star? Politician? I get off, there's cheers. Guy steps forward, says, "Mr. Pot-kin, we are glad to have you back." Must have been 25 media people at the airport, snapping pictures, doing interviews.

I do the weekend, they lose both games, they didn't like me as much.

There are so many intangibles, so many different factors involved beyond my control, that I never can tell in advance how the act will play. Lopsided ballgame, bad weather, lousy acoustics, so many things can go wrong.

And if a fight breaks out, I'm dead.

Like the night in Daytona, when Al Campanis's son was catching for Daytona. The pitcher hits him, he runs out and decks the pitcher. Both benches empty, a brawl breaks out. The act was ruined.

One of the worst fights I ever saw happened in Calgary during a doubleheader—Billings against Calgary, sellout crowd—even the owner got involved. The umpires threw both catchers out and Billings forfeited. Then the owner wanted to fight with the Billings manager. It was brutal.

Another memorable fight happened in Midland, Texas, a double-A game against Jackson. I'm supposed to coach in the third inning. Jackson gets seven runs in the first inning. That team was loaded with guys who went up with the Mets, including Kevin Mitchell.

Mitchell hits a homer and a triple in that first inning. Second inning, it's 15–0. The Midland manager says something racial to Mitchell. Mitchell looks into the dugout, says, "You can have a piece of me anytime."

The manager rushes out, Mitchell decks him, boom, one punch. Now both teams rush onto the field. The crowd is incensed, and it's my job to make 'em laugh. I go out there, third inning, first guy up gets drilled. Both benches empty again. Me, I lay down, head on the bag, like it's a pillow while the fight goes on. My act died.

Sometimes, even after careful planning, after hours of preparation, something can go wrong, because the players involved weren't listening. Or, caught up in the intensity of the game, they simply forget their parts.

Take that time in Eugene. Billy Champion was the pitcher. I used to include a little catching routine in my act. I'd walk up there with a glove and motion for the pitcher to throw me three pitches.

The first pitch, I'd exaggerate the catcher's crouch to where I was practically on the ground. He'd throw a blooper and I'd take a swan dive forward and the ball would go over my head. Second pitch I'd just snatch at, and gesture that I wanted him to throw harder. Third pitch he'd throw hard. I'd pretend to hurt my hand, I'd get angry and throw the ball and the mitt back at him.

Well, that night in Eugene, I'm crouched for the first pitch. I swan dive forward like I'm supposed to, but Champion forgot the routine and throws a 90 MPH fast ball. It sails just past my head and hits the backstop with a thud. It was supposed to be a blooper. If it had hit me between the eyes, they'd have scraped me off the plate with a butter knife.

You see, lots of things can happen while I'm out there on the field, while the game is going on. That's one of the things that sets me apart from the ducks in almost every big league ballpark now—I call them "ducks" because they all waddle in those big costumes, whether they're supposed to be a chicken or a parrot or whatever it is the Phanatic is supposed to be in Philadelphia.

I like Dave Raymond, the guy inside the Phanatic costume. He's a good, young guy with a lot of energy. But sometimes he goes too far.

I remember when Lonnie Smith was with the Cardinals and Smith got tired of being mocked by the Phanatic stumbling around under make-believe fly balls. Smith tackled him, put him out of action that night.

And there was no reason for him to get involved in a scuffle with Tommy Lasorda. He smashed that dummy in a Dodgers uniform in front of their dugout and he knew Lasorda would react and he did. And then he kept the feud going, smashing Los Angeles batting helmets, the whole bit.

There's one bit that the Phanatic does that annoys me. I imagine it annoys a righthanded hitter even more. The Phanatic gets up on the Phillies dugout, first base side, and he jumps around, trying to put a hex on the opposing pitcher. The guy at the plate, trying to concentrate on the pitcher, can't help but see this fuzzy green thing jumping around out of the corner of his eye. It has to bother him.

The Chicken is a duck of another feather. He came along at the right time. I'm from the old school. I make a decent living, but compared to what he's making, the newsboy cashes my check.

He badgers the umpires, something I never do. He unfolds those eye charts and he imitates them and makes fun of them if they're heavy. He even mugs a dummy dressed in umpire's clothing. And he gets raunchy at times, with the female fans.

I appeared in the same ballpark with him back in 1986, when Louisville owner A. Ray Smith booked us for the opener against Buffalo. The Chicken used all that loud music and props. Me, I went out there, in uniform, and did my thing.

Chapter 12

GEORGE BUSH, STRAIGHT MAN

Ballplayers, umpires, managers, they all dream of the big leagues. They get stuck in the minors for too many years, they quit, go home, get another job. Me, I've worked the minor leagues for 50-something years, hanging on to the thought that someday I'd get some national exposure, some big-time recognition.

Maybe it's not meant to be.

Pat Williams, the general manager in Orlando now, hired me once when he was with the Philadelphia 76ers. The Celtics were coming to town, nationally televised game and Pat booked me to perform at halftime.

I had a nine-minute baseball skit that Mickey Shaugnessy had given me, and I was excited—World Series game, three guys get on, how I get out of it—all pantomime.

That day, Chet Forte, who was directing the telecast, told Williams he had interviews set up at halftime and that there was no way I could do the skit.

Pat asked me if I could cut it down, and go on, just as soon as the first half ended. I rush out there, it seemed like I was on for about five seconds. Who cared about baseball in the middle of a Sixers-Celtics game? I ran through the skit. Forte was mad, because his guys had to talk over me in the background.

But the all-time disappointment happened in Cincinnati, at the major league All-Star game. Bob Howsam, a real good friend I had dealt with in Denver for many years, had become the general manager of the Reds. Cincinnati had the All-Star game and Howsam told me I'd perform as part of the pre-game show.

I get out there, I've got Dave Zinkoff as my announcer.

I go into the clubhouse, put my uniform on, and then I walk into the dugout. Pete Rose was there, and I remember he was sitting near Danny Kaye, the movie star.

Rose said, "Wait 'til you see this guy, he's funny as hell."

President Richard Nixon was coming to the game and Secret Service guys were swarming all over the place. But his plane was late. Out on the field they had a bunch of little kids in some kind of cockamamie pitch-catch-throw competition. Now, suddenly, here comes Dick Wagner, who worked for the Reds. A real gloomy, hatchet-man kind of guy. He says to me, "Max, the kids used up your time, Nixon is late, you're not gonna be able to perform."

My heart sank. Wagner says they'll announce me, I can come out and take a bow. I realized it was never meant to be. They had never advertised that I would be there. They had not even put my name in the pre-game notes they handed to the press. When I got to Cincinnati, there was no hotel reservation waiting for me.

I'd been double-crossed. I sat in the clubhouse with tears in my eyes, peeling off the uniform. They threw me a bone, sent me a check, but it never made up for the sadness I felt.

Jim Barniak, who died too young, was working for the *Philadelphia Bulletin* back then. He came over, interviewed me, wrote a story. I had to be in Albuquerque the next day. I got there, and my brother Eddie phoned me. He said that Barniak had written a beautiful story about me. That helped a little. It was one of the worst things that ever happened to me. I'm still not sure why it happened, who decided that I couldn't go on.

Years later, The Chicken was booked at the All-Star game in Seattle. But they didn't want him on the field, so he roamed around the stands. The act died. They don't need entertainers at an All-Star game, although in '93 they wound up with Michael Jordan and Tom Selleck in a home run hitting contest and I'm not sure what that was all about.

The Super Bowl, they go nuts. Michael Jackson at half-

time, 4,000 kids with hula hoops, smoke and noise, and
jet fighters overhead.

It would have been nice, doing my thing on a big
stage. Lord knows I've played enough small stages. But I
can't complain, really. I've brought laughter into so many
ballparks, met so many warm, wonderful, fascinating
people.

Like the fat madam in Klamath Falls, Oregon. She ran
a house of ill repute. Came to most of the home games,
bringing three or four of her best-looking girls, including
a stunning redhead that caught my eye.

She loved the game and she had a standing offer,
anybody on the home team who hit a home run got a
freebie at her place. Burt Convy, who became an actor
and a game show host, he was on that team. Vinnie
DeCarlo was the manager. I got to town, asked him how
the club was doing. He said, "We're leading the league in
homers."

I told him the guy who led the team in homers would
have to crawl back to his hometown when the season
ended.

Me, I didn't get a freebie. The redhead made me pay $5.

Over the years I've played all kinds of venues and with
all sorts of people—and not always with people! I worked
with a seal act in New York. Sharky the Seal, terrific act.
He worked on a platform and then he'd slide into the
water, spin the ball on the end of his nose. I've followed
dog acts, even an alligator act at another show. You follow
an alligator, the stage is all slimey and smelly.

Years ago, my agent got a call from the Johnny Carson
show, asking if I was available for a certain date. I was
scheduled to be in Montana that day, so I turned it down.
That ranks right up there with the dumbest things I've
ever done.

After the movie *Bull Durham* came out, somebody from
the David Letterman show called me. He started asking
me questions, how I got started, the whole bit. We talked
for about 10 minutes. He wound up saying, "We'll get

back to you." Which is the kiss of death in show business. A week later, he called, said they decided not to use me. He said I didn't sound too funny on the phone.

I wasn't trying to be funny, I was just trying to answer his questions.

Charles Kurault did a nice show featuring me on the road. They showed it on a Sunday morning, early, before most of my friends were even awake. Maybe I'm not classy enough for prime time?

I remember when the State Department sent me over to help entertain troops in Europe, and we got to France. On a day off we toured Versailles. I'd never seen a joint with so many rooms in my life. We're touring this bedroom, and they say that that's Josephine's bed. I jump over the railing, plop on the bed, and yell, "How about this, I'm in the same bed that Josephine slept in."

The guards came, chased me out of the room, chased me out of the palace.

And I've worked in sports other than baseball. I toured with the Globetrotters. Eddie Gottlieb, who was acting as my manager, was a good friend of Abe Saperstein, who owned the Globetrotters. In those days, Gotty supplied the team that played against the Trotters. They were the Philadelphia SPHAS. Later on, it was the Washington Generals, coached by Red Klotz.

The SPHAS had Jerry Rullo, Tookie Brown, Lennie Weiner, Elmo Morgenthauler, and a guy named Bill McCahan, who once pitched a no-hitter for the A's. It was all one-night stands in those days and we traveled from place to place in cars. I'd sit in the back seat, playing gin rummy with Lenny Weiner, who played at Southern High but never went to college.

The Trotters are a great act, but it wasn't that much fun for me. I did a little baseball comedy skit at halftime. But I have to say that Goose Tatum is the funniest man I've ever seen. He had those long arms, and a unique gait and a voice that made people laugh. All his routines were choreographed.

They had Marquis Haynes, who was probably the

world's best dribbler, and Sweetwater Clifton, who wound up driving a cab in Chicago when his playing days were over.

They bounced that ball around to the tune of "Sweet Georgia Brown," and they did the gag with the bucket full of confetti that the audience thinks is filled with water. Tatum had that baseball routine, where he'd hit the basketball with his fist, and then run around the bases, like he'd hit a home run.

And they always had a halftime show of different acts, like the world's best ping-pong player—a guy from England. And that's where I came in. I did my baseball skit at halftime, lasted about seven minutes. I was never really comfortable doing a baseball skit as part of a basketball game and there were nights I felt I was banging my head against the wall. Mickey Shaughnessy, who was a great nightclub comic, gave me the act. He loved to appear in Wildwood, a good guy, a funny guy.

On my first tour with the Globetrotters, I'd play sometimes with the SPHAS. One night, we beat the Trotters in Rochester. Saperstein went nuts. He screamed at them. They'd won 100 games in a row. They've probably never lost since. It was just one of those nights, the game was close, they got a little careless, and we beat them.

There was a time when the Trotters had to play straight basketball. They'd tour with an All-Star team, college guys who hadn't signed with the pro teams yet. One year, that All-Star team had Walt Bellamy, Bill Bridges, and Dave DeBuschere. Cab Calloway was the featured band at halftime, and he'd stand there, rooting against that All-Star team.

Those games drew big crowds and the fans saw good basketball. And a good show at halftime. Those were the glory days for the Trotters. They've gone downhill since then, been sold three or four times. Once Meadowlark Lemon left to form his own group, they lost some of their luster.

Basketball doesn't hold that many fond memories for me. Unless you count that night in St. Louis when I was playing in a media game, a warmup to the regular NBA game that night. I got ready to go into the game, I pulled off my sweat pants. Trouble was, I pulled off my shorts, too.

Come to think about it, I didn't have too many memorable moments in football either. Bill Veeck was friendly with Carol Rosenbloom, who owned the Baltimore Colts then. He booked me at an exhibition, an intrasquad game, for the benefit of the Police Athletic League.

I'm supposed to appear at halftime, but I've got nothing planned. Weeb Ewbank was the coach. They kick off, Lenny Moore runs it back 100 yards, and that was the only touchdown. Game ended, 7–0.

Halftime, they've got Arthur Donovan, Big Daddy Lipscomb out there. I've got a helmet on, shoulder pads, a shaggy uniform. I'm running into Donovan. He says, "I'll knock you over, you knock me over."

Then, they put a barrel out there and I'm in a passing contest with Johnny Unitas. He misses one. It's best-of-three. I'm milking the hell out of it, and I throw one right into the barrel.

Now, I'm kicking against Bert Rechichar. He misses one on purpose. It's my turn. I tell the guy to move the ball in closer to the goalposts. I work my shoe loose. I run towards the ball, he yanks it away, my shoe goes through the crossbar. The official signals "good." The crowd goes crazy.

Another time, the Green Bay Packers had an intrasquad game. I was in Green Bay to perform at a baseball game. Pete Reiser managed the team then. There's a timeout in the football game, the announcer introduces me, figures I'll give a sample of what I'm going to do at the ballpark that night. I go out there, I'm clowning. Vince Lombardi screams, "Get that crap off the field."

Hey, you can't please 'em all.

I did get to work with a president, George Bush. Actually, he was running for vice president at the time, and he was in Denver, campaigning. I was there with a major league, old-timers All-Star team that included Willie Mays, Mickey Mantle, Warren Spahn. Must have been 15 Hall of Famers on that team.

We had appeared in Buffalo, Indianapolis, and now we were playing Denver. Bush was staying at the same hotel as the ballplayers, so there were lots of cops outside, and so many FBI guys and Secret Service guys swarming in the lobby.

One of Bush's top aides came up to me, started to tell me his brother had played baseball with me somewhere along the line, and that he would see that I got my picture taken with Bush at the ballpark. We get out to the ballpark and there's a huge crowd, at least 40,000. I was going out there in the fifth inning. And just then, the gate opened down the rightfield line and here came this huge limousine.

The limo drives right up to the dugout and out steps George Bush. He's wearing a Denver Bears uniform. The public address announcer says, "Ladies and gentlemen, now playing first base, the Vice President of the United States, George Bush."

Now, there are security guys ringing the dugout, and guys standing near the box seats with ear pieces in their ears.

It's my time to work the first base coach's box. I go out there, there's some guy standing there with a Bears uniform on. I look at the guy, he's got a huge bulge in his pants.

I say to him, "Is that a gun, or are you just glad to see me?"

The guy glares at me, and says, "It's a weapon, and I'm here to protect the Vice President in case some nut comes out of the stands."

I'm used to working alone. I bet there's never been a time with two coaches in the box, and neither one of them a real coach.

Meanwhile, Bush is throwing the ball around the infield. He's a lefthander. I'm stuttering and ask him how he feels about being my straight man. He says, "Sure, I'll be your stooge."

We did the routine where I mimic the first baseman, we hadn't rehearsed, the whole thing was a surprise. So, I'm whispering to him to take off his hat, and he does it.

I tell him to stretch his arm, and he does it... Finally, the inning ends, we get a big hand, and now he goes to bat. He got a base hit off Spahn, I remember that. The crowd loved it.

After that, in the dugout, a guy grabs me, tells me to stand with the vice president, show him something about hitting. So that's when I got my picture taken with him. He told me he used to watch me perform in Texas. He played first base at Yale, he was a legitimate fan. And he had a home in Texas, so he probably saw me in Houston, or Austin. They sent me the picture. And years later, when he was elected vice president, they sent me an invitation to the inauguration. I've got it framed.

They also sent along a request for a donation. You don't send $100 to the White House. So, I figured it out, with renting a tuxedo, the plane fare, the hotel, it was going to cost me $1,000.

I decided to pass. As it turned out, it was a great decision. That was one of the coldest Januarys on record in Washington, and they moved most of the ceremonies indoors. But sometimes I second guess myself. If I had gone to Washington, I would have jitterbugged at the Inaugural Ball. That might have put me in the fairy tale books, right alongside Cinderella.

Chapter 13

HOORAY FOR HOLLYWOOD

Appearing in the movie *Bull Durham* put new life in my career. Which is funny, because I was supposed to die in the original script.

Annie Savoy, the woman played by Susan Sarandon, asks me why I go on all these years.

And I tell her, "Annie, I love this game of baseball, I truly love this game."

And then I ask her to do me a favor. When I die, I want to be cremated and my ashes spread at home plate. The ballclub can put some of my ashes in the rosin bag, so I can stay in the game. Touched, she leans over and plants a kiss on my cheek. When I talk about it now, I say, right after that, she threw up.

Anyway, in the film we're sitting at a table in this nightclub and the waitress brings over drinks. We say we didn't order them and she says, "He did" and she points to Crash Davis, played by Kevin Costner.

I holler, "Crash, come on over here." And then I introduce them, "Annie Savoy, Crash Davis."

An argument starts, Crash and the kid pitcher go outside, to fight, she's dancing with me. (I had to teach her the jitterbug routine.) Then, I pass the bus, driving out of town. I'm clowning, waving to the guys. Later, word comes that Max Patkin has run into a train. They send my ashes to her, she stages a memorial service at the ballpark, and you see Timmy Robbins, the pitcher, with the rosin bag in his hand.

They took the dying part out and what's left, I guess, is me doing the spray on the field, some stuff coaching first base, and the nightclub scene where I introduce Annie and Crash.

People tell me it's a great movie. I still haven't seen it. I just don't like to look at myself.

It turned out to be a terrific baseball movie because a baseball guy wrote it, Ron Shelton. In the 50's he was a minor-league player for Stockton in the Cal State League. I performed, and afterwards, he was one of the guys I asked to come with me. We sat around, had a few drinks. I guess he remembered, because out of the blue I got a call from a producer saying that Ron wanted me in a movie he was making.

I handled the deal myself, didn't use an agent. Probably short-changed myself. Got $5,000 plus royalties—hey, I'd have done it for nothing.

It was the off-season, I wasn't doing anything. I got down there, walked on the set, Kevin Costner came over, said, "Max, I've heard a lot about you, I'm happy to see you in this picture." That made me feel good.

And Susan, she was adorable. Looked good. Nice body. We'd do a scene, she was supposed to act serious, but she kept grinning. I guess she'd never seen a face like mine. One day, they brought us real beers in the nightclub scene. That didn't help me remember my lines, so they wrote them down on the coasters

They brought me out to Hollywood for the premiere. Wound up staying in a Century City hotel, The Westin, best hotel room I've ever had. It cost $800 a day, had a Jacuzzi bigger than most rooms I'd ever stayed in.

There were seven telephones in the suite. I called my brother, Eddie, started telling him about the room. He said he was flying out from Philadelphia, just to see it. He said he'd bring his camera and take pictures. He flies out. Sure enough, he forgets the camera. What's the good of being a Patkin if you can't be scatter-brained? Wouldn't buy one out there. Too cheap. But it was great.

I'd been thinking about quitting my act, because my knees were hurting so much. But when the movie came out, and more people recognized me, it was like a spark to keep the fire going.

Soon after, I'm in the Charlotte airport, waiting for a flight. The captain comes by, spots me, says, "You're Max Patkin, I saw you in *Bull Durham*, you were wonderful."

I get on the plane, I'm sitting in coach, where I always sit. The stewardess comes by, says the captain would like me to be his guest, in first class. I move up to first class, the captain gets on the intercom and says, "This is your captain speaking, we have one of the stars of *Bull Durham* on board, Max Patkin, the Clown Prince of Baseball."

The kids scrambled around, came up to me for autographs, it was great.

I'd never really seen a good baseball movie. The baseball scenes are always too corny, they're not realistic. I love Jimmy Piersall but that *Fear Strikes Out* movie was terrible. Even *The Lou Gehrig Story* was tough for me to watch because of the baseball scenes. And the worst I ever saw was William Bendix playing Babe Ruth.

I'd had some experiences with Hollywood before, and most of the experiences were bad.

Once, a long time ago, I was in love with this girl I met in California. She didn't care that much for me. But I thought I'd like to stay in Hollywood, be a dancer. People had been telling me I ought to be in pictures. My face, my style of dancing, they thought I'd be great in movies.

One time, Bill Veeck and his wife, Mary Frances, were out there. We were at a place where Red Nichols and his band were playing. I'm showing off, dancing up a storm. I remember Veeck unscrewed his wooden leg and laid it on the table.

This guy comes up to me and says, "I'm Busby Berkely and I love the way you dance."

That encouraged me. The president of one of the studios was related to my uncle, so I got in to see him. He watched me dance and then he said, "You're too Jewish-looking."

I am, and proud of it. But that ended any ideas about a movie career. Hey, it worked out for the best. Hollywood spoils people.

Take Johnny Beradino, who used to be my closest friend on the Browns. He's an actor, appears regularly in "General

Hospital." I wouldn't trust Beradino to put a Band-Aid on my finger, and he's acting as a doctor. He has no time for ballplayers any more. Last time I called him, his wife said, "He's not in," but I know he was there. I can't remember him doing anything remarkable as a ballplayer, but Bill Veeck, in *The Hustler's Handbook*, recalled the celebration that followed the World Series championship.

"John clambored onto a table," Veeck wrote, "struck a suitable dramatic stance, and, stopping only occasionally to quaff from the bottle in his hand, proceeded to declaim from the works of Shakespeare.

"He ran the gamut from *Othello* to *Henry V* to *Romeo and Juliet*, playing all parts himself, a virtuoso performance. Let it be carved upon his Emmy: Good Lear, No Hit."

I remember a charity softball game I played in. Joey Bishop, the comedian from Philadelphia, was in it, and Allen Gale, Jerry Lewis, and Dean Martin. Lewis was playing first and Martin was pitching. I'm in the first base coaching box, imitating Lewis, everyone is laughing. He turns around, real serious, leans down and whispers, "Okay, kid, you've had enough, get the hell off the field."

I come in the dugout, I'm hurt. I tell the ballplayers. They say, "Get the hell back out there."

I go out, do my stuff, and Dean Martin backs off the mound, laughing his butt off.

Sammy Davis, Jr. was part of that famous "Rat Pack," but my first encounter with him wasn't too pleasant. I knew this girl singer named Mickie Marlow, who worked at Ciro's. She said that Sammy Davis was having a party at his house in Coldwater Canyon and she invited me to come along. I remember Sammy's father was in the kitchen. I had seen the Will Masten trio, so I knew who he was.

Mickie and I were in line for drinks, but there was music and Mickie said, "Let's dance." So, we start to dance, in the living room. People are laughing, because I'm doing my eccentric jitterbugging. And suddenly, this big guy, six-five, at least 260 pounds, steps out and says, "Be no dancing here!"

Who am I to argue, so we stop. But people are telling me they want to see me. I'm flattered, so we start to dance again.

Out steps little Sammy Davis, Jr. He puts his finger up, under my nose and says, "My man told you, no dancing!"

I say, "It's your party," and we stop.

Now that I think about it, my first experience on a Hollywood set, should have convinced me that I wasn't meant to work in motion pictures. I was with Cleveland then, and one of the club owners was also president of Universal Pictures. He cleared it for us to visit some movie sets.

Me, Al Lopez, Bob Lemon, Lou Boudreau, went out there. Saw Ava Gardner on the set of *Singapore*. Met Burt Lancaster, who was doing *Brute Force*. And then, we met Peter Lawford and June Allyson, who were making *Good News*. That time, Jackie Price was with us. Well, he gets to meet June Allyson and he lets this snake come out of his shirt. She's tiny, and suddenly, she's face to face with this snake peeking out of Price's shirt. She screams, runs off the set. The director chased us.

One of the best things that happened to me in Hollywood was meeting Johnny Weismuller. I met him while playing in a golf tournament in Whittier. Weismuller was in our foursome, me, Peanuts Lowery, and Hank Sauer. I'm clowning around, the way I always do, and Peanuts and Hank are getting pissed off because they're trying to win the championship.

Weismuller loved me. He had such a good time that day, he gave me a set of golf clubs. First good set of clubs I ever had. I don't know whether to thank him or not, because I wound up playing more golf than I should have, for more money than I should have. I'd never taken a lesson in my life, just grabbed the clubs and started hitting. Wound up with a lot of bad habits that way.

I was just too stubborn, too proud, to admit I needed lessons. And I never wore a golf glove. I liked the feel of the grip in my hands. Never wore a batting glove either. I thought gloves were for sissies. Now, you've got big league ballplayers wearing batting gloves on both hands, and sliding gloves when they get to first base, and a glove inside their mitt when they're playing the outfield.

Weismuller gave me his phone number, invited me to come visit him. The next time I came to town I called him, and he invited me out to his house. His wife winds up doing my laundry, washing out that mud-stained uniform. I wanted to do something nice for them, so I invited them to the Slate Brothers, a nightclub where my good friend Don Rickles was performing.

Weismuller is half-gassed and we're right up front. Well, Rickles cut him to pieces and Weismuller was hysterical. Rickles is doing Cheetah, all the stuff from the Tarzan movies Weismuller had done, jumping up and down, scratching himself.

He takes his encore, Rickles leans over, says in a loud whisper, "Don't worry, Max, I'll introduce you."

Rickles is a great guy, big heart. I was at this fund-raiser for the Child Guidance Clinic recently with Larry Bowa, Mike Schmidt, and Garry Maddox. I was wearing a yellow turtleneck. Rickles spots me, hollers, "There's Max Patkin, he looks like a Jewish parakeet."

Me, I'm not a standup comic. I can't stand there on a stage and tell jokes. I can't do a pre-game act. I have to be involved in the ballgame, interacting with the ballplayers, the crowd, the umpires.

I did appear on the "Chase and Sanborn Hour," way back in 1946. With Zasu Pitts. That was the first live variety show televised around the country. I did "You Asked For It" with Art Baker. And I appeared as myself on "To Tell The Truth," the show where a panel had to guess the real Max Patkin. I brought three uniforms and they put the other two on two very normal looking human beings. I couldn't believe it when only one panelist, Peggy Cass, guessed me as the real Max Patkin.

And then they asked me to show them some of that "Rock Around the Clock" routine and I started dancing. I threw my leg up over the moderator, Garry Moore. I was a little leg weary and I just barely got my leg up over his head. Good thing he wore one of those severe crewcuts, otherwise I'd have messed his hair up and knocked his glasses off on national television.

When I first started out and I was touring with the Enos Slaughter All-Stars, we got to the West Coast and Leo Durocher asked me to go on his television show. It was called "Double Play" and he was on with his wife, Larraine Day. They sat on a set that looked like their living room.

Larraine said, "I have a player who plays any position. His name is Max Patkin." I come out, Leo asks about my pitching arm. I pitch, pretend to catch, play the outfield. It was a seven- or eight-minute bit.

There was a time when someone talked to me about appearing in a Broadway musical based on Bill Veeck's life. A guy spent weeks talking to Veeck about his adventures, but nothing ever came of it.

And some people who said they were connected with Dick Van Dyke talked to me about a movie based on my life, but that went up in smoke. I'm not sure Dick Van Dyke was good-looking enough to play me.

I wound up on the cutting room floor in my only other big picture adventure. Gene Kirby, a television producer with a good baseball background, was the technical advisor when Robert Redford made the movie, *The Natural.*

They were shooting it in Buffalo and they needed someone to warm up the crowd. Hey, it was after the season, people were sitting there and you could see the breath coming out of their mouths, so they really needed someone to warm up the crowd. (I have to tell you that some of the fans were really cardboard cutouts.) Anyway, they played a simulated game and I did my stuff as the comic coach. The director got a kick out of me, and said he'd try to work me into the movie. So they put me in a scene, dancing on the top of the dugout, but later they changed their minds.

But I got $2,500 for one day's shooting, which was nice.

Then my brother had a heart attack, which was not so nice. He wanted a hot dog and I wouldn't get him one and he got all upset and pretty soon he had this pain in his shoulder and he wound up in the hospital with a heart attack.

He's had five heart attacks and he's in frail health. I worry about his days being numbered. When he comes with me, on short trips, he sits in the car.

I tell him it's because he doesn't think I'm funny anymore, just to needle him. But I know that he doesn't like to see me out there, struggling, 73 years old, trying to make people laugh, doing all the physical stuff.

Chapter 14

BUMPED BY AN UMP

I love umpires.

I don't know if umpires love me, because I'm out there clowning while the game is going on. They're trying to maintain law and order and I'm thrashing around in the coach's box, flinging dirt on myself.

I depend on the umpires—to let me do my thing, to go along with the last bit I do, diving into third base. The good guys call me out, argue back when I argue, throw me out with a flair. The guys who are tired of the travel, depressed by the low salaries, homesick, lonely, they go through the motions with me. That's okay. I understand because I've spent so much time in the minors myself.

The saddest, scariest episode I ever saw was in Appleton, when I was pitching in the Wisconsin State League. The umpire made a call that went against Appleton. Tough call.

The game ended, and when I came out of the clubhouse, there was that umpire, up a tree.

The fans had waited near his car, and then chased him, and he scrambled up this oak tree. He was a Jewish umpire, I remember that, but I can't recall his name. There must have been 100 people surrounding that tree. It looked like a lynch mob. Two Keystone Kop guys were there in uniform, helpless. Finally, they got reinforcements and the crowd was dispersed.

It's a tough grind, umpiring in the lower minors. Two-man crew, bad lights in a lot of ballparks, low pay, and not much respect from the players and managers. I've seen guys who didn't have the stomach for it quit in midseason. And I've seen guys stick it out. It pays to stick it out, because the guys who get to the big leagues are well paid now, with vacations during the season, with tremendous benefits.

All that security, all those perks, have caused some umpires to be complacent, to skip the conditioning that goes into doing the job right. Some of them are overweight. But none of them compete with Scotty Harris, an umpire I ran into while performing. He must have weighed 375 pounds.

In those days I was doing the bit where I'd kick off my shoe, smell it, faint. Well, I kicked off my shoe and it landed right on top of Scotty's head.

The crowd kind of gasped because they didn't know what was going to happen next. He motioned me to walk towards home plate. He had that serious look on his face. He motions me to come closer, closer... He gets up in my face and then... Bam! he bumps me with his belly. I was so shocked, he knocked me on my keister. The crowd loved it.

Looking back, I learned an important lesson about umpires early on. It was 1948, I was still feeling my way, looking for stuff to make people laugh. One night, I got behind the home plate umpire, pretending to call balls and strikes, exaggerating my motions.

A guy named Johnson, I forget his first name, was in the stands that night. He was the umpire supervisor for the Midwest League, had been a triple-A umpire himself. He sent word that he wanted to talk to me.

He said, "Max, I can get you banned if I give the word. I know you're out there trying to make a living, but you can't humiliate my umpires. You've got to leave them alone.

"The job is tough enough without you badgering them. I'll let it go this time, but I don't ever want to see it again."

From that day on, I never embarrassed an umpire. I shouldn't say never, because, sometimes, while I'm out there, I lose track of my resolutions. Like that exhibition game at Wrigley Field in Los Angeles. Al Barlick was behind home plate. He had this high-pitched voice, like chalk on a blackboard.

I'm coaching first base and I start imitating his calls, "Steeerike One."

I do it three or four times. He whips off his mask, stomps down to first base, and hollers, "You're gone!" He had never seen me before because he was a National League umpire. He didn't know I clowned around. So he thumbed me.

We traveled by train in those days, and the umpires rode with us. Now, Al Lopez, who was a great agitator, tells Barlick, "Max says you're horseshit."

Barlick comes looking for me. He says, "I'm gonna punch you out." Finally, Lopez told him he was only kidding around. Barlick became one of my good friends. He's retired now, and he'll come to see me when I play Springfield.

Jerry Neudecker, who's retired now, was umpiring in the Southern League when I met him. He was telling me how he was taking this correspondence course to be a certified public accountant, because he wasn't sure he was ever going to get promoted. In walks Al Sommers, an umpire supervisor, a guy who had his own umpire school. He asks this ump which school he went to. The guy tells him. Sommers frowns, walks out. The guy turns to me and says, "I think I'll study harder."

Sometimes, hitching rides with umpires won't get you very far. John McSherry, who has added a few pounds since I first met him, was umpiring in the Carolina League. He was going to drive me back to the motel in Winston-Salem after the game. But he had a tough game and when we went out to his car, there were two ice picks in his tires. And the other two were already flat.

Riding with umpires can also be risky. There was one time in Puerto Rico, a big game in Ponce, because Ponce was tied with Santurce for first place in the Winter League. Luis Arroyo was managing Ponce, and he didn't want me to go out there because it was such a big game. He told me, "If we lose, with you flapping your arms like a seagull, they'll kill me."

But Ponce took the lead so Arroyo let me go out there. I gave it my best stuff and the crowd went crazy. Guys were throwing their straw hats onto the field. I lost track of the curtain calls. So I'm feeling great and now I catch a ride back to San Juan with the umpires. One of the guys has a date and he's driving too fast around those mountain curves. We go around one curve, doing 45, and bam! there's a pack of wild dogs on the highway. The guy swerves, we almost go over the side of the mountain.

Along the way I'd met Gertrude Geara, who was trying to become the first woman, big-league umpire. I was performing at West Palm Beach and she was going to umpire school there. She came over, interviewed me. She was doing a story for her hometown paper—I think she only lasted one day on the job.

Pam Postema was a different story. I must have worked 30 games with her and I thought she was a competent umpire. I used to kiss her at the end of my act. I asked her first if it would be okay, and she gave me permission. She was tough. She had to be, to handle the abuse the players gave her. I thought she had a good chance for making it to the big leagues. I understand she's suing baseball for gender discrimination, and she wrote a book about her experiences.

Chapter 15

Not So Golden Earrings

When Casey Stengel was managing the Mets, he once moaned, "Can't anybody here play this game?"

Casey was right. People who know the game are horrified by what they see going on in big-league ballparks. Me, I'm not surprised, because I see what's going on at the minor-league level, how guys swing at bad pitches, how guys swing when they ought to be taking pitches, how outfielders can't hit the cutoff man.

And you ask a guy to bunt today, you might as well ask him to sing opera—in Italian!

You mention fundamentals to today's players and their eyes glaze over, like you're talking some foreign language. Players just want to swing the bat, pile up individual statistics. They moan if the manager flashes the 'take' sign, three runs down in the late innings.

I suppose some people will say that a clown shouldn't be criticizing the state of baseball, but I've been part of the game for almost 50 years, and I think I know how the game should be played.

I don't like the way a lot of so-called superstars look these days. I don't like beards, I don't like that long hair dangling down to a guy's shoulders. I don't like all that gold jewelry hanging around a guy's neck. And I especially don't like earrings on a player. Barry Bonds might be a great player, but it makes me sick to see that gold earring bouncing around every time he goes to the plate.

I remember, years ago, I ran into Phil Cavaretta in a hotel lobby. He had managed for years and suddenly quit. I asked him why he quit.

He told me he had this kid in Visalia who had gotten a big bonus to sign. The kid broke one of the rules and

Cavaretta said he was going to fine the kid X number of dollars.

He says the kid looked at him and said, "I'll get your job before you get my money."

Cavaretta said he wondered what had become of respect and that's when he decided to quit.

I saw lack of respect first hand one winter in Puerto Rico. I was doing a show on the last day of the regular season. A doubleheader was scheduled, but the rains came pelting down and the first game was pushed back until 6:30.

A guy named Wilfredo Calviño was managing the team. He posted the lineup card on the wall and Reggie Smith was in the lineup. He walked over, grabbed a pen, and crossed his name out of the lineup. Calviño asked him why, and he said there was something wrong with his leg. They argued, squared off, but people got in between them. They lost the doubleheader and didn't make the playoffs. From that time on, Reggie Smith never liked me. He'd ignore me whenever our paths crossed.

Reggie later played for Tommy Lasorda. People think Lasorda is a story-teller, a guy who hangs out with Hollywood people, a guy who shmoozes the media. They don't really know him. Under that funny outside, there's a tough competitor inside. I found that out the first year Lasorda managed, in Ogden. He had a pretty good team there with guys like Bill Russell and Steve Garvey and Ron Cey.

They're winning a game by seven runs and they blow it. I'd done my coaching bit for Ogden that day, and now I'm in the clubhouse trying to get dressed, because I've got to catch a bus for Salt Lake City. It had to be one of the smallest clubhouses I've ever seen. Slightly bigger than a phone booth. And now Lasorda is chewing them out for losing the game. It's over 100 degrees in there and he won't let anybody get dressed, he won't let anybody out of that clubhouse. Parents are waiting outside, girlfriends are waiting outside, and Lasorda is scorching the walls with his language.

Even in the Navy, I had never heard language like that.

Nowadays, if a manager tried to lock his players in the clubhouse for an hour after the game, there'd be a mutiny.

Davey Johnson got fired by the Mets, and he was out of baseball for years. He got back with Cincinnati. I wonder if he wishes he had stayed retired. The fish don't give you backtalk. He got into it with Kevin Mitchell over discipline. The year before, Lou Pinella scuffled with one of the Cincinnati pitchers in the clubhouse.

Guys are making so much money now, they're harder to discipline. The Players Association protects them, so a manager has to be careful if he fines a player.

Guys are making so much money, they forget the time they spent in the minors. It's an attitude that bothers me, because I knew them when they were getting $5 a day for meal money.

The summer of '92, I had an open date after a Midwest League appearance. I called Ron Schueler, the general manager of the White Sox, and asked if he'd leave me a pass. He did, and I got on the bus taking the Baltimore Orioles out to the ballpark. Not one guy on that bus said hello to me. I walked towards the back of the bus, nothing.

It really burned me up. I walked into the clubhouse with them, and as I was getting ready to leave, I turned around, and said, "Not one of you sons of bitches even asked me what I was doing in town, or how I'm doing."

One of the guys, a real wise guy, said, "What are you doing in town, Max?"

I glared at him, and I said, "Go screw yourself." I was really angry.

They say it's easier to fire a manager than to get rid of 25 players. That explains why the Mets fired Jeff Torborg. My good friend, Dallas Green, couldn't do much with that mob of underachievers.

I think some of this stuff started in pro basketball. Magic Johnson got Paul Westhead fired in Los Angeles after Westhead had won the championship in his rookie year as a coach.

And Michael Jordan got Doug Collins fired in Chicago after Collins had helped get the Bulls on the right track.

There's a new breed of owners in pro sports, and they don't have much patience. Which is why you see so many general managers getting fired, too.

Baseball is far behind basketball, though, when it comes to promoting its superstars. In the NBA, you see Jordan's face everywhere. Charles Barkley shows up with Godzilla in commercials. That Olympic "Dream Team," that was pitiful, those guys moaning about the outfit they were supposed to wear to the gold medal ceremony, and then hiding the label by draping an American flag over it. Shaquille O'Neal came into the league, and before he even played in a playoff game, his face was everywhere.

In baseball, all you ever hear are owners squawking about how much money a guy is making, and whether he's earning it or not. And the players don't go out of their way to relate to the fans either.

You get a creep like Vince Coleman who throws a firecracker towards a crowd waiting around outside Dodger Stadium. And for days he can't bring himself to say he was sorry.

You've got guys making big bucks doing autograph shows, charging $15 to sign something. Demanding the money in cash. That's the kind of action that got Pete Rose in trouble with the IRS and put him in the slammer.

I think all those huge contracts contribute to all the brawls that happen when a pitcher throws high and inside to a hitter and the hitter rushes out to the mound.

These guys aren't used to getting thrown at because they use aluminum bats in college, and pitchers don't throw inside. And when they get to the big leagues, they don't want to risk those big paydays by getting nailed by some pitcher who wants to reclaim the inside part of the plate. One guy gets hit, he expects his pitcher to retaliate. The guy who retaliates gets tossed out of the game. A fight starts, somebody gets hurt at the bottom of the pile.

Maybe they ought to copy hockey and punish the third man in. Let the pitcher and the hitter fight it out with nobody else involved. That might stop all the bench-emptying brawls (It was something when Robin Ventura decided to go after Nolan Ryan. He went out there, Ryan got him in a headlock and hammered away, six punches to the noggin.)

While I'm sounding off on the things I don't like about the game today, I have to include the two-faced rule about no tobacco-chewing in the minor leagues, while nothing is done about guys chewing and spitting in the big leagues.

A guy like Lenny Dykstra, good player, tough player, walks up there with a wad of chewing tobacco in his cheek. He's already had surgery on a lip damaged by snuff, but he gets to keep on chewing. But in the minors, guys sneak off for a smoke in the clubhouse or grab a quick chew between innings. It's sad.

I don't like beards, long hair, earrings. I don't like guys loafing to first base. I don't like guys who make excuses. I don't like guys who wind up on the disabled list with a hangnail.

In the old days, guys had one-year contracts. Even on teams that were hopelessly out of the pennant race, you'd see pitchers begging for that extra start, so they could squeeze in one more win. You'd see hitters battling that last time at bat, trying to fatten their batting average.

They called it a "salary drive" in those days, because they wanted to have decent numbers to take to the table when they haggled with the general manager during the winter.

Now, you've got arbitration, maybe one of the worst changes in baseball in the last 50 years. Some college economics professor, who doesn't know a bunt from a bagel, decides whether the player should get the $3.2 million he is demanding or the $2.8 million the club is offering.

And that's for your .260-hitting shortstop.

Expansion has diluted the talent. When the National League expanded into Colorado and Florida, it added 20 pitchers to the big leagues that would have been in the minor leagues.

And I don't like ballplayers justifying their enormous

salaries by pointing out that Frank Sinatra makes $100,000 for a one-night concert, and that movie stars get paid millions for a lousy movie.

They say they're entertainers!

I'm an entertainer, they're ballplayers, part of a team game. Some of those guys, they couldn't spell team if you spotted them the t-e-a. They have a responsibility to the owner who's paying their salaries. They have a responsibility to their teammates. They have certain obligations to the fans who buy the tickets—who pay for their outrageous salaries.

Chapter 16

DANCING IN THE DARK

People are always making suggestions about what I can do with my act. These are well-meaning people. I'm not talking about the grumps whose advice usually involves an obscene, impossible contortion.

I've had all sorts of suggestions down through the years. One that crops up time and again is dancing on top of the dugout.

There's a couple of problems there. First, it's hard to find a good partner in some towns. What I do is jitterburg, and today's kids don't really know how to jitterbug. They're into disco, hip-hop, all that free-style thrashing around. Secondly, some ballparks have such lousy sound systems, it's tough to keep time to the music.

What I do, is bring along my own tape of "Rock Around the Clock," the old Bill Haley number. The guy who wrote the lyrics was Jimmy Myers, who played bit parts in the movies. He belonged to the Philadelphia Athletic Club, which is where I got to know him.

I did a charity event at Broad and Olney for handicapped kids. His band was playing there, and he gave me permission to use "Rock Around the Clock" in my act. The public address announcer says, "Max, show us some of that rock and roll pitching form" and he puts the tape on. I do a minute of rock and roll dancing in the coach's box and then it's time to play ball again.

Pretty straightforward routine. Only, one night in Charlotte, the PA announcer slapped the national anthem on the tape player instead, and everybody was standing at attention while I'm out there ready to rock and roll.

The dancing comes easy after all these years. I taught myself to dance, growing up in Philadelphia. I was ahead of my time. Years later, Dick Clark made a whole career out of "American Bandstand" using Philly kids on his television show. I appeared on the very first show. A disc jockey named Bob Horn was the host. (He got in trouble later on, messing with some teenagers.)

They staged the show at 46th and Market. The producer had seen me at the Click, a downtown nightclub owned by Frank Palumbo, and booked me.

I'd win champagne sometimes, in dance contests, and I'd give it away. If I won a trophy I'd forget to bring it home. And when there was prize money, it was five or 10 bucks and I'd spend it before the night was over. It was the excitement I craved, being up there, in the spotlight. I remember I'd go over to Pennsauken and dance at Neil Deegan's nightclub. I'd dance with the chorus girls.

Sammy Kaye was one of the bandleaders who played the Click, and he had this routine where he'd ask "Do you want to lead a band?"

He'd get volunteers out of the audience, and they'd stand up there and wave the baton. The audience would pick the best "bandleader" and he'd get a prize. One night I went up there, went through my gyrations, got a big hand. I remember that Frank Palumbo gave me a case of champagne for winning the contest.

I got to know the bandleaders. In some cases, it took a little while for them to warm up to my act. Like that time in Hollywood, Gus Zernial and I went to the Palladium. Harry James was the hot band at the time. I'm jitterbugging and a big crowd forms to watch me. Here come two big bouncers and they growl, "No exhibitions allowed."

Exhibitions? I was just doing my normal jitterbugging. So I keep on dancing. Next thing I know, they've got me by the armpits and they're dragging me towards the door. Zernial is hollering for them to put me down. They put me down, all right, after they tossed me out the door.

It turned out that Harry James loved baseball, and later, we became good friends.

Once, when I was dancing at the Click, Vaughn Monroe came in. I was up there, on stage. He sent word that he wanted to talk to me. He said he was on tour, stuck for an act, because somebody had gotten sick. He said he needed me for a week or two. The money wasn't that great, but it was something new, so I took the job.

We toured New England. Played four shows a day in Hartford. He was at the top of the Hit Parade in those days with "Racing With the Moon" and "Dance, Ballerina, Dance." What I'd do is dance with the Moon Maids, his singing group. Each one would take turns, cutting in, as we jitterbugged.

When I was with the Browns, I lived at the Chase Hotel. That was the hot spot in St. Louis, with top-notch entertainment playing in the ballroom atop the roof.

I was up there one night with Johnny Beradino, my teammate.

(When I knew him, as a ballplayer with the Browns, he was Berardino. Maybe, when he got to Hollywood, he droped the "r" to make him better looking? I remember the Philadelphia Eagles once drafted an offensive lineman named John Brooks. When he got to training camp, he told the writers he was spelling his first name J-o-n. They asked him what had happened to the "h," and he said he'd dropped it to make him faster.)

Xavier Cugat was the featured band and Abbe Lane was his singer. She'd invite people to come out of the audience to cha-cha with her—cha-cha or rhumba, and occasionally, jitterbug, which started with the Lindy in New York. They're playing a jitterbug number and Johnny shoves me onstage to dance. I start dancing with her, and suddenly, I throw my leg over her head.

She'd never seen anything like that, so she screamed, and she turned and ran off stage.

The crowd thought it was funny. They're applauding and Cugat is standing there, embarrassed. He starts motioning for Abbe Lane to come back out there. She's hiding in the wings and she refuses to come back out.

The story gets back to Bill Veeck, who owned the Browns and loved the Chase Hotel. He calls J.G. Taylor

Spink, the publisher of the *Sporting News* and invites him to come watch me. He winds up reserving two big tables, 16 people. And he gets word to Cugat that I was a coach and a comic and a good dancer. Cugat convinces Abbe Lane that it's okay and she finally relents, comes out, and dances with me.

People kept telling me I could make a career out of dancing, but I had that one depressing tryout in Hollywood, on a movie set, and I knew that a movie career was not for me.

The dancing comes in handy, during my baseball act, as a change of pace. Most of what I do is pantomime, yet I can't stand to watch mimes perform. I can remember once, in Chicago, I was doing the ice show at the Hilton and Marcel Marceau was performing across the street at the Blackstone. I contacted his public relations man and asked if I could have my picture taken with him. He turned me down.

I doubt he ever came to see me do my pantomime skit at the ice show. Puggy Sluka, the famous, gravel-voiced public address announcer, did the background commentary.

The scene was the seventh game of the World Series. Ninth inning. I'm out there in relief. I've got an earned run average of 92.7. I lean in, act like I don't like the sign, shake it off. Wham, a line drive goes by my face. Puggy says I may be hurt, but I shake it off.

Here comes a slow ground ball, oops, it goes through my legs.

Next guy hits a pop fly, the catcher calls for it, waves the infielders away, oops, it drops safely. Now the bases are loaded. I get two strikes on the hitter, I turn, wave to the outfielders, calling them in. I wind up, I pitch, wham, the guy hits it 500 feet.

It sounds simple, but it was tough work. By the time I finished the act, I'd be puffing.

I did a similar act when I toured with a "Baseball Celebrities" troupe in 1953, performing for GI's in Europe. The master of ceremonies would introduce me. "Here," he'd say, "is the handsomest fellow in baseball, Max Patkin."

The GI's loved it. I'd do this skit, pretending to be a pitcher facing the New York Yankees. I'd be out there, struggling, trying to get out Phil Rizzuto, Billy Martin, Yogi Berra, and the other Yankees.

I'd argue with the umpire, give up a bases-loaded homer to Berra, and then trudge to the showers.

Chapter 17

HALL OF FAMERS

Satchel Paige once tried to explain how he lasted so long as a pitcher. He listed six simple rules, but he left out his real secret, which he confided to me in the shower one day.

Paige pitched professionally for more than 40 years. His rules have become famous:

1. Avoid fried meats, which anger up the blood.

2. If your stomach disputes you, lie down and pacify it with cool thoughts.

3. Keep the juices flowing by jangling around gently as you move.

4. Go very light on the vices, such as carrying on in society—the social ramble ain't restful.

5. Avoid running at all times.

6. Don't look back. Something might be gaining on you.

All good rules, but that day in St. Louis, when Paige was with the Browns, I saw him standing under scalding water in the shower. He told me that that was his secret, running very hot water on his pitching arm after he pitched.

He said he'd built up immunity to the scalding water. I tried to step under the shower and I couldn't stand it. Nowadays it's all ice, ice, ice. A guy pitches six innings and they wrap his arm in enough ice to sink the Titanic.

Satch was amazing. They'd applaud him just walking in from the bullpen. He had that confident way of walking. A strut, almost. He'd take the ball from the manager, throw two or three warmup tosses and say, "I's ready!"

By the time he got to the big leagues he must have been 38 years old. I saw him pitch in Philadelphia when

I was a kid, back in the 30's. He never told anybody his real age. It just added to the mystery of the man.

I remember one day , he was with the Miami Marlins, when he pitched against Bob Kuzava in the Orange Bowl. There were more than 50,000 people there. I'm finishing up my act. He's supposed to throw the first one in tight, and he does, at about 80 MPH.

The next one is down the middle, and I fall on my keister. The third one, he's supposed to throw it slow enough for me to hit it somewhere.

This one he throws 90 MPH. I yell, "Easy, throw it easy."

Here comes another blazer, 90-plus. I'm screaming at him and he's scowling back at me. He throws another unhittable pitch. I throw the bat at him, run to third base.

Afterwards, he said, "You ain't gonna hit me."

I think about Paige, I think about the time he came to Philadelphia to pitch against the Kansas City Monarchs. He was pitching for the Pittsburgh Crawfords at that time.

I didn't go inside the park that day. I waited outside, on Spruce Street, hoping to catch a foul ball. If you caught one, they'd give you a dime, and take the ball back inside. I didn't want the dime, I wanted a baseball. And sure enough, here came a foul ball. I ran it down, caught it. And now, two guys start chasing me. They want that ball back. They chased me for five blocks. Finally, I ducked into the backyard of a house and crouched under the cellar steps. I stayed there for five hours, until it got dark.

I kept thinking, if I come out, they'll be there, they'll grab the ball back. And I wanted that ball. Not to keep, not to get autographed. I wanted that ball to play with. And when we wore the cover off that ball, we went to the hardware store and bought a roll of black friction tape and wound that around the yarn and played some more.

Paige was just one of the Hall of Famers I've gotten to know down through the years. You're out there for six decades, you're going to cross paths with some great players. Some of them were great guys too. And some of them were lousy human beings. It's interesting that the baseball writers added a rule that takes into account a player's integrity and character when they're voting for the Hall of Fame. If you kicked all the drunks and skunks who are already in—out of the Hall of Fame, you'd have a lot of empty spaces on the walls.

I remember the first time I saw Pete Rose, in the low minors. Somebody told me to watch this guy. He drew a walk, he ran to first base. Faster than some guys run on a base hit. Me, I happen to think Rose belongs in the Hall of Fame. Got more hits than anybody who ever played the game. Talked about it all the time, like an ambassador for the game. Hustled all the time, even in a meaningless All-Star game, like when he crashed into poor Ray Fosse at home plate.

If you judged Rose on what he accomplished on the ballfield, there's no doubt he belongs. They never did prove he bet on baseball. The commissioner, Bart Giammati, said he did, after he and Pete signed a paper saying that they wouldn't claim that Pete bet on baseball.

Giammati died soon after of a heart attack, and some people even blamed Rose for that, which is unfair. The next commissioner, Fay Vincent, was Giammati's best friend, so he certainly wasn't going to reinstate Pete. If Rose stays out of trouble, I think somewhere down the road, by the year 2000, he'll be reinstated, and the writers will vote him into the Hall of Fame.

Talking about Rose reminds me of Johnny Bench, who *is* in the Hall of Fame. I see him at charity golf tournaments. Good guy. I guess the first time I ran into him was in Buffalo, during that batting routine I do at the end of my act. I crawl through the catcher's legs. I remember how solid he was.

Mickey Mantle had to be one of the greatest players I've ever seen. If he hadn't torn up his knee stepping into that sprinkler hole at Yankee Stadium, he might have put up numbers that would be out of reach. Mantle came from a family where the men died early of leukemia. Mickey jokes about it now, but he means it when he says that if he'd known he'd live this long, he'd have taken better care of himself.

You can't mention Mantle without mentioning Willie Mays. When there were three teams in New York—Giants, Yankees, Dodgers—the papers were always arguing about who was the best centerfielder, Mays, Mantle or Duke Snider. Some guy wrote a song about that, called "Willie, Mickey, and the Duke."

Mays could do it all—run, throw, hit, hit with power. He might have stuck around a year or two too long. He'd lost a step or two. Part of it was ego, part of it was the money was starting to get good.

Dizzy Dean was one of the first guys voted into the Hall of Fame. He belongs. It was funny listening to him on television, working with Buddy Blattner. Diz mangled the English language, but people loved it. He was a hustler, for all that rube image. He hustled in golf, he hustled in gin rummy... (as I found out on one expensive plane ride from St. Louis to Philadelphia.)

My first hero was Jimmy Foxx, but I never really got to know him. How was I to know that as the years went by, I'd be on the same ballfield with guys like Warren Spahn, Ernie Banks, Bob Feller, Joe DiMaggio?

Spahn was managing in Tulsa, in triple-A, when I was coaching third one day. Tight game, Tulsa losing by one run, and I sent a guy in—he was out by a mile.

The batter had gone to second on the throw. Ordinarily, I look into the dugout, ask the manager, can this guy run? This time, I forgot to ask. The guy had a bad leg. Another base hit, I send the runner, bingo, he's gonna be out so far, he stops. They get him in a rundown, tag him out.

Spahn screamed at me, "You've gotta be the worst third base coach I've ever had in my life!" But he wasn't really that angry.

First time I ever saw Henry Aaron, he was in Eau Claire, playing second base. Like a lot of people, I couldn't believe the wrist action on this guy. I didn't know he'd break Babe Ruth's home run record, but I could see, even then, he was going to be a great hitter.

I first met Ernie Banks when he was playing with the Kansas City Monarchs. Even then he was enthusiastic. When he played for the Cubs, he'd always be chirping, saying, "Let's play two," and, "Welcome to the friendly confines of Wrigley Field." I know that some of his teammates called him FOS, for full-of-shellack, but I can't judge him. He was a good guy, and seemed genuinely excited about playing the game.

Joe DiMaggio wasn't voted into the Hall of Fame the first year he was eligible. That's just one of the mysterious things about the voting. There are some guys in there voted in by the veterans' committee that didn't come close to getting enough votes in the 15 years they were on the regular ballot. Makes you wonder, because they sure didn't get any more hits, or strike out any more batters, after they were dropped off the ballot, and before the old-timers got to vote on them.

DiMaggio was a great player. Maybe he was unappreciated because of the graceful way he played the game. Maybe he made it look too easy.

DiMaggio is a very, very private person. You've got to be very careful what you say around Joe because he's so sensitive. I'm in awe of him. And even though I tell the story about how I got started doing baseball comedy by chasing him around the bases in Honolulu, I always talk about how far he hit the ball.

The thing that amazed me about Joe was his baserunning. I don't know if you could look it up, but I get the feeling he was safe 99 percent of the time he went from first to third, .

DiMaggio worked for Charlie Finley for a while. That must have been tough for Joe, because Finley had all these whacky ideas. One year, when the Oakland A's were in the World Series, Finley brought the jackass mascot into the media dining room.

For years, DiMaggio was content to do the Mr. Coffee commercials. Later on, he represented a New York bank. But you didn't see him going around, selling his autograph or doing any schlock commercials. That was before the

Home Shopping Network started selling baseball memorabilia. Now, they've got autographed DiMaggio bats for $3,995. That's an expensive piece of lumber.

They said he was only going to sign 1,941 bats to signify the year, 1941, when he hit in 56 consecutive games. Joe is still very popular, because he has this dignified personality, but almost $4,000 for a bat seems a little steep.

Bob Feller deserves to be in the Hall of Fame. But the two years we were together in Cleveland, I doubt if he spoke 10 words to me—was a little egotistical. Everyone knew about Feller's fastball, but he had one of the best curves I've ever seen.

I remember, my first season with the Indians, 1946, we were playing Detroit and 50,000 showed up because Feller needed two or three strikeouts to break Cy Young's all-time strikeout record. It started raining and now Hank Greenberg is the hitter. He takes a half-swing and the umpire says, "Strike three, you're out."

I shouldn't knock him, I guess, because I made some good money barnstorming with him in the off-season. He took Jackie Price and me with him in '47, and he paid us $100 a game, which was good money in those days.

Feller earned his money, pitching every day for 30 days, because the fans came out, expecting to see him. He had his wife along, so we had to watch our language.

We played tough teams. We played the Harry Walker All-Stars in Birmingham. We got to the West Coast and played the Kansas City Monarchs. When Satchel Paige pitched against Feller they filled Wrigley Field in Los Angeles.

We played one ballgame in a bullring in Mexico City. When we got to Tampico, there were railroad tracks across the outfield. The train would chug from leftfield to rightfield.

We're playing the game, we hear the train whistle. Here comes this work train. We look at it, there's Jeff Heath on the caboose, waving his shirt, hollering "Viva." The train went out the other side of the ballpark, we had to wait for Heath to run back to his position in leftfield.

In '51, I toured with the Enos Slaughter All-Stars. Slaughter had to wait a long time before he got into the Hall of Fame. He blamed it on biased writers, some of whom probably never forgave him for the way he reacted when Jackie Robinson broke the color line.

Fido Murphy, who used to be a scout for the Chicago Bears, promoted that tour. I remember we had to line up in the hotel hallway after every game to get paid. Guys like Spahn, Slaughter, out in the hallway, waiting to get paid.

One of my favorite Hall of Famers is Al Lopez. I think I'm as close to Al as anybody I've ever met in baseball. He joined the Indians as the second-string catcher in '47, but I truly believe that Veeck intended to name him the new manager. One of the papers ran a ballot, asking the people to vote whether they ought to keep Lou Boudreau as the manager or fire him. Well, the response was overwhelming. People wanted to keep Boudreau.

Lopez and I became close friends, not that you'd know it that time in Sacramento, when he nearly got me killed in a bar. Bob Lemon, Jim Hegan, Lopez, me, and three or four others, were in this bar. I was having a Coke. In walked Pat Seery. Lopez decides to needle him. He tells him, "Max is standing here, telling us how you were his 'out' man when you played for Appleton and he was in the Wisconsin State League."

Seery goes nuts. He screams, "That big-nosed son-of-a-bitch could never get me out. I'll show him who's an 'out' man."

It took five guys to hold him back.

Years later, in Chicago, Lopez invited me into the clubhouse. They'd just lost a tough game and here came a herd of writers. Lopez said they'd have to wait, he wanted to talk to his good friend, Max Patkin. He just wanted to stall them, but he made them wait, while he talked to me.

Rogers Hornsby, he fired me after he became manager of the Browns. He was one of those purists who hated my act, although he did like to watch me dance.

They'd fired Zack Taylor to name Hornsby the manager.

I like to say that the Browns in those days abused the privilege of being lousy. I'd sit next to Zack and I'd suggest strategy. So here's this clown sitting next to the manager, telling him he ought to do this, do that. The ballplayers would laugh. Finally, one day, Zack turned to me and said, "You do the clowning and I'll do the managing."

I sulked, slumped off to a corner of the dugout, sat there brooding.

Around the fifth inning, Zack turns to me, says, "Why aren't you going out there to coach?"

I said, "You do the managing, I'll do the clowning."

We had a sad club. We did have Ned Garver, who won 20 games, and that was on a team that lost 100. Garver was good enough to bat in different spots in the lineup. Once, he even led off.

Last day of the regular season, they've brought Hornsby in to be the new manager. Augie Busch had bought the Cardinals, and Veeck was afraid that they were going to hire Horsnby as their manager. So Veeck beat him to the punch and hired Hornsby. They stage a big press conference, and later on, he's in the press box, surrounded by writers and radio guys.

He looks down at the field, and I'm out there clowning in the first base coaching box. He points at me, and says, "That big-nosed son-of-a-bitch, he's gone!"

Hey, at least I got fired by two Hall of Famers, Lou Boudreau in Cleveland and Hornsby in St. Louis.

Hornsby wasn't the only Hall of Famer who disliked me. Joe Medwick hated my act, although he never said so to my face. I found out because one of the scouts told me that when he sat behind home plate and I was performing, he'd say, "Get that crap off the field, it's making a mockery of the game."

A genuine Hall of Famer was Stan Musial. Great hitter, terrific guy away from the ballpark. I wound up touring with him once. He'd bring along his harmonica, play "Red River Valley" all the time. He was good, but not great. Larry Adler didn't have to spend any sleepless nights worrying about Musial's harmonica playing.

I always wondered why it took them so long to vote Bob Lemon into the Hall of Fame. He definitely belonged. I pitched against him in the Navy. He beat me twice, 5–1 each time. He hit a home run in each game and drove in six runs. Played third base before he pitched.

Johnny Mize, who has passed on, was another Hall of Famer I pitched against. Johnny Lucadella was our second baseman. I turned around and he was playing about 10 feet in front of the rightfielder.

I yelled at him, told him to move back where he belonged, on the infield dirt. He yelled back, "I don't have enough insurance to play that close."

Baseball lost two great guys about a week apart in '93 when Roy Campanella and Don Drysdale died. I first met Campanella when he was playing in Nashua. He truly believed that you had to have a lot of "little boy" in you to play the game. I got friendly with Drysdale after his pitching career was over. He did a lot of radio, and he was always nice to me. Not like today's players; most of them won't even acknowledge me when I come into the clubhouse.

A month later, Reggie Jackson was inducted into the Hall of Fame. He's from Philadelphia, and he belongs— for all the clutch home runs he hit, for the flair he brought to the game.

Somebody told me years ago that Jackson could tell you the pitcher, and where the ball landed, for every one of his first 100 homers. That's amazing.

When I look at the list of Hall of Famers, and realize I've worked with so many of them, it makes my head spin.

Paul Waner, he wound up scouting for the Braves and I'd run into him in the minor league parks. Everyone knew he loved to take a drink. He once told me about how he'd go up there, see three baseballs, and swing at the middle one. Said he didn't mind when it looked fuzzy, because it looked bigger that way.

Early Wynn, he had a reputation for being tough. He'd

say he'd knock his own grandmother down, and then add, "But she was a pretty good hitter." For all that toughness, he's one of the leading guys in trying to get benefits for the old-time players who aren't covered by the pension plan.

Mel Ott, he enjoyed my act. He came up with the Giants when he was still a teenager. Had that unique batting style, where he'd raise his front foot before swinging. He's the guy who was managing the Giants, when Leo Durocher said, "Nice guys finish last."

Harmon Killebrew, the slugger, people don't associate grace with him, or a sense of humor. But he might be the best first baseman I ever worked with, when I do that shadow routine. I'd whisper for him to yank his hat off and he'd do it, wipe his brow, stuff the cap back on his head. He was smooth, and the crowd loved it.

I'm still not sure whether the sportswriters ought to have that paragraph about judging a guy's character and integrity on the ballot. Me, I judge people by how they treat me, but I wouldn't rule a guy out of the Hall of Fame just because he's a jackass.

Take somebody like Bob Gibson, a terrific competitor, a great pitcher, but a grump. I walked into the trainer's room when he was with the Cardinals once, and he was laying there. He said he didn't want to listen to any of my crap. I started to fire back at him, but I looked over and Joe Torre was standing nearby. He gestured to me, put a finger to his lips, motioned for me to leave quietly. So I did.

The other side of that coin is a guy like Carl Hubbell. King Carl Hubbell. Became famous when he struck out five American Leaguers in a row in that All-Star game. When I think about him I remember playing golf with him in Johnstown, Pa. He was farm director for the Giants then. He shot two over par. I was lucky to break 100. He was a nice guy, humble for all he had achieved. The Giants let him go when ownership changed.

When I think about guys who belong in the Hall of Fame, I often think about Ernie Lombardi. There's a catcher who hit .300 and never got an infield hit in his career. He had a big nose, like me, and we called him "Beezer." Some guys called him "Schnozz." I call him unlucky, because he wound up working in the press box at Candlestick Park.

I'm already on record as saying that Pete Rose belongs in the Hall of Fame. I think Leo Durocher belongs there too, as much for what he accomplished as a manager, than as a player. Sure, Leo was loud, profane, a bragger. Maybe he even said, "Nice guys finish last," which is the saying he's most famous for. But he cared about winning and he cared about the game.

One other guy who belongs is Orlando Cepeda. He had some great years with the Giants and the Cardinals. If you just look at his lifetime batting average, his homers, you know he belongs.

He did make that one serious mistake, getting involved in a shipment of marijuana to Puerto Rico. He served his time, paid the penalty. But he's changed his life around, does good things in the community.

You'd think the writers would forgive and forget.

Cepeda once told me that he thought I belonged in the Hall of Fame. My sister wrote a letter to the Hall of Fame people asking about it and they wrote back saying there was no category for entertainers.

USA-Today carried a little story about it and a guy named David C. Mohr, from Lehighton, Pennsylvania, wrote the selection committee a letter and sent me a copy.

"Please be reminded," Mohr wrote them, "that a whole generation of us 'baby boomers' who love baseball grew up secure in the knowledge that Mr. Patkin was out there, somewhere, entertaining and sharing his deep love of the game with, by now, countless fans.

"Since you have a special Honor Roll of Baseball to honor men for 'outstanding contributions to baseball other than by active playing,' I would greatly appreciate if you would consider recognizing one of the greatest assets baseball has ever had, whatever his category, and place Max Patkin's name in nomination for the Baseball Hall of Fame."

I understand the business about categories, but they've got that Abbot and Costello routine, "Who's on First," featured at Cooperstown and those guys never wore a uniform.

I've put in a lot of years in baseball, not as a mascot, not as a circus performer. I put in time as a player in the minors, as a coach on the major league level, and then, almost 50 years as a performer.

Maybe, some day, if there are enough guys who have seen me through the years on the veteran's committee, they'll find a place for me.

Chapter 18

THE CUSTOMERS ALWAYS WRITE

You need thick skin if you're going to be a clown.

People figure they can't hurt the feelings of a guy who looks like I do. They figure I've heard every insult known to man, that I have squelched hecklers from ocean to ocean, that I'll have a quick comeback prepared, or that I'll just shrug and smile and walk away.

Often, after I've finished my act by the fifth inning, I'll shower, dress, and walk into the stands while the clubhouse guy is washing my dirty uniform.

I'll usually sit with the scouts, who gather behind home plate, with their clipboards and their stopwatches and now, radar guns. (I don't know about radar guns, ever since I aimed one at a tree and caught it going 50 MPH.)

Ben Wade, who was one of the top scouts for the Dodgers back in the 50's, was sitting there one day, with Dolph Camilli and some other guys, must have been 10 scouts there.

Wade turns to me and says, "Max, I've been watching your act for a long time, how about sending me your schedule for next year?"

I fall right into the trap and I say, "Why would you want it now?"

And he says, "I want to know where you're going to be, so I can avoid your act."

He was just teasing me, but I should have given him my schedule, just to show him how many miles I cover. Sometimes, it was crazy. In 1987, I flew from Philadelphia to Anchorage to Vancouver to Portland to Honolulu to Nashville.

Five shows in five days.

And, until I tripped on those clubhouse steps in Fenway

Park in August, 1993, I never, ever, missed a performance because of injury, illness, or personal problems.

The problem with being so durable is that nobody realizes when I'm hurting. It happened in Phoenix one year, in 1987, at a reunion for the 1962 Los Angeles-San Francisco playoff teams.

I got distracted, started choking on a chunk of steak. I'm sitting there, gasping, turning blue, and everybody at the table thinks I'm joking around, playing for laughs. Finally, some guy out of the audience came over, used the Heimlich maneuver, grabbed me and squeezed, until I coughed up the piece of gristle.

Of course, some of the problems I've had, I caused myself. Like the time I decided to buy a tear gas pencil. I didn't need it for protection, I just wanted to see how it worked. I was in the clubhouse in Richland, Washington. Billy DeMars was the manager. I fired it against the wall and blam, the whole clubhouse was filled with tear gas. The guys had to dress outside. Luckily, DeMars was a teammate when I was with the St. Louis Browns, so he forgave me.

Once, in Chicago, I was bragging about my new contact lenses. I was sitting on the bench, before the game. Someone asked me how I got 'em out and I showed them—you just pop it out.

I pop it out, it falls in the dugout and now I can't see without it. I've got Nellie Fox, Walt Dropo, and Al Lopez looking for it. The game is set to start and I'm still hunting for the contact lens. Bill Summers was the plate umpire. He grabs Lopez and tells him he's got to get me out of the dugout. We held up the game for five minutes. Finally, Nellie Fox found the lens.

Another time, in Hollywood, I was out with Buddy Lester (the comedian), Chuck Connors, and Johnny Beradino. I pop one out, I show them how you put it back, resting it on one finger.

I was supposed to dip it in water, but it falls off my finger and into the glass. The glass is almost full, so I decide to drink some of the water.

Bingo, I swallow the lens.

They cost $180 a pair in those days. I had to get a fresh pair from Dr. Bernie Simmons, the eye doctor in Philadelphia who took care of a lot of the athletes.

Now, my day begins with eye drops to fight glaucoma, a pill to keep my blood pressure down, I can't eat before a performance, and if things don't go well, I can't eat after a performance.

Despite all the places I've been, I've never really been any place. I played Niagara Falls, but I never went to see the Falls. When I go to a town, I go from the airport to the hotel to the ballpark to the hotel, and back to the airport. I don't sight-see. Now, with so many motels out near the airport, I sometimes don't see the town at all.

When I started, you didn't have a television set in every room. You had the Gideon Bible in the dresser drawer and you had a little radio alongside the bed. I'd fall asleep listening to the radio. And before I fell asleep I'd study the train schedule or the bus schedule. I wish I had a dime for every hour I spent in some smelly bus station.

And I had it easy compared with the black ballplayers in the South. There were separate water fountains for blacks, separate men's rooms. The black, minor-league players had to really want to make good, considering the conditions they had to endure. They'd have to take a bus ride to the other side of the tracks while their white teammates stayed in the one good hotel in a town.

I've caught my share of bigotry, too. Overhead a fan once talking about a black player, saying, "He's nothing but a Jew turned inside out." Fought a teammate in the Wisconsin State League who called me a "dirty Jew." And there was that brutal bus ride from Kinston to Durham, when I got a bigot kicked off the bus.

There couldn't have been more than 12 people on the bus, lots of empty seats. I remember this German couple was on the bus. The guy sat in one aisle seat and the girl sat across the aisle. I had the seat in front of the girl.

Now, an older man gets on, and he slides into the seat

next to the girl. Plenty of empty seats, but, no, he takes that one. That made me wonder about the guy.

And now, he starts talking to her, and I can overhear the conversation, and I don't like the way it's going. He seems to be leading up to something.

He says to her, "Do you like Jews?"

I spin around. I tell the guy I've been listening, and I'm not gonna give the woman a chance to answer. I tell him he had no business taking that seat in the first place.

Now, the bus driver gets involved. He had heard parts of the conversation, and he didn't like the way it was going. He stops the bus, walks up to the guy, and orders him off the bus. I felt good about getting involved, even though I'm not a crusader. I'm a clown, I'm supposed to make people laugh. I leave the serious stuff to the serious people.

I read the sports sections of the papers in every town. One of the nicest things ever written about me was a column Jim Murray did in the *Los Angeles Times*, back in 1973.

Murray used that line from Veeck about how it looked as if I'd been put together by a guy who couln't read the instructions very well. And then he wrote:

"Someone had started at the top, and finished in the middle. For one thing, they forgot to put the bones in. He looked as if they found him on a broomstick in a cornfield.

"He was 6–3, but 30 percent of that was neck. He had two miles of arms, and his face looked like the world's biggest hunk of bubblegum.

"The nose rose out of it like Mt. Whitney out of an aerial photo. His neck was so long he could read over two guys' shoulders and, when he wound up on the mound, he had to be careful his two arms didn't send the rest of him somersaulting like a guy caught on a propeller.

"He was a guy who could be funny just standing still. He twitched constantly like a guy having a bad dream. Some guys have a nervous tic in the eye or the mouth. Max had one all over.

"He was 6–3, 140 pounds of nervous tic. He looked as if he had a permanent case of the hiccups. His ears should have had lights on them.

"But Max wanted to be Bambino, not Bozo. The history of show business shows that almost everyone would rather get laughs than cheers. And Max didn't need a script, a nose that lit up, a seltzer bottle or a fire hat."

People wonder why I endure the loneliness, the grind. The laughter.

It keeps me going. Seeing fathers bring their kids to the ballpark to see me. Guys shouting out to me, how they saw me years and years ago.

I've had checks bounce. I've had general managers stiff me. I've seen general managers who won't spend a quarter to publicize or promote my appearance, then whine about the crowds I draw. In the beginning, I worked on percentages. But I had to give that up when I was getting so many strange counts. I'd look around, there'd seem to be 5,000 in the ballpark and the guy would say he'd drawn 3,000.

I didn't have anybody checking the turnstile count, how could I argue?

So, after that, I set a fee, with a rainout fee. The Chicken's rainout fee is about what I charge to perform, but I'm not complaining. As long as I'm getting bookings year after year, I want to keep going. When the bookings die or when the laughter stops, that's when I'll stop.

It's strange, the way some of the guys who resented me at the start are now some of my best friends.

Frank Dolson, the columnist for the *Philadelphia Inquirer*, he's a purist. I'm sure that the first time he saw me, he said, "Get that garbage off the field." But down through the years, he has become a good friend. He's a guy I can call from the road, when I'm really down, and he'll listen.

I guess I've won over about 95 percent of the baseball people I have to deal with. They realize I'm out there simply trying to earn a living. I help draw some people to the ballpark, I make people laugh...

And one other thing, I don't hurt anybody.

I look around, I don't see anybody to take my place when I hang 'em up. Who's going to work the days I work, the schedule I work, for the money I've been getting?

The mail I get is amazing. A typical letter says, "I first saw you perform at a Eugene Emeralds game in 1972. That same night I saw Greg Luzinski, Bob Boone and Mike Schmidt. Looks like you outlasted them all!

"Last week I took my third daughter to see your act at a Portland Beavers game. All three of them loved every minute of it. Thank you!

"My oldest daughter collects autographs but was not able to get yours when you were in town. Could you please sign the enclosed card for her? Thanks again!"

I'm always amazed that mail addressed to Max Patkin, King of Prussia, Pa., gets to me.

A retired Army guy living in Germany, working as a teacher at the American High School in Stuttgart, wrote to me:

"I'm no youngster myself, 66 last July, but have been a lifelong baseball fan," he wrote. "I saw you perform on two different occasions and can truthfully say you were great!

"I guess the real proof of your greatness was that I can't even recall who played and the outcome of the games, but I do remember Max Patkin's performance!"

When I toppled down those steps at Fenway Park, sprained my ankle, and ended my 50-year streak of never missing a game, I got mail from all over America. Included in the mail was a "get well" card from Logan W. Hurlbert, director of the Great Falls Dodgers. "We will always remember the landing on the moon, won't we?" Hurlbert wrote.

Doug and Mary Grace Scribner of Rio Rancho, New Mexico wrote, "Heard about your fall at Fenway Park. Hopefully you are all right! Thank you for making us laugh. We are your biggest fans in New Mexico."

Evie and Chuck Murphy of the Florida State League wrote, "Be sure to get in shape at the winter meetings as no one can dance the way you do!"

Adam Bonfiglio of Rockaway, N.J. wrote, "I hope that you'll be up and about soon, and so do all baseball fans. You are a true gift to this wonderful game and have warmed many hearts and I hope you continue to do so for many years to come."

One of my favorite cards came from John Garofalo. He wrote, "Your recent setback gives me the excuse I shouldn't have needed to tell you how much sheer, absolute, unmitigated joy you've brought to me and my friends over the years.

"I saw you just a couple of weeks ago in Portland and laughed my ass off, as always. We met a few times when I was in the Braves system in the late '50s, early '60s, and I've never forgotten the warmth you communicated when you weren't performing, as well as the many times you helped me forget my troubles and remember that—*it's just a game*! Get well soon."

I got a letter once from a doctor at Mercy Hospital in Omaha. A doctor named John F. Fitzgibbons. It was a terrific letter. I remember he said that there is a special blessing in heaven for a man who makes kids laugh.

Maybe it sounds hokey, but that's what keeps me going.

Chapter 19

THE PEN IS MIGHTIER

I don't think they've put a rabbit in the baseball, but there are times when I hold the ball alongside my ear and can hear a faint heartbeat. How else can you explain all those little-bitty guys hitting those long home runs? The ball seems to leap off the bat these days and head for the bleachers to become a souvenir for the fans—except in Wrigley Field, where they toss back homers hit by the enemy.

The manufacturer swears, on a stack of record books, that the ball is the same, same center, same yarn, same stitching, but I have trouble believing it. Which is why I have trouble when people tell me that Barry Bonds may be the greatest player to ever play the game.

Better than Willie Mays? All Mays could do was hit, hit with power, run, throw, catch, and cover more ground than those Mississippi floods.

Better than Roberto Clemente, who died too soon? Clemente could hit to all fields, with power. He could run, had a rifle for an arm.

I usually dodge whenever anyone asks me to pick out the greatest hitter I've ever seen—or the best pitcher, the smartest manager, etc. Times have changed, travel has changed, ballparks have changed, and I'm convinced the baseball has changed, too. Let's just say that I think Willie Mays is one of the best players I've ever seen—and I started out, as a kid, seeing Ty Cobb.

Steve Carlton was one of the best pitchers I've ever seen. He could throw that nasty slider with the count 3-and-2, and get it over for a strike. And if it broke low, and out of the strike zone, the hitter might take a timid, half-swing at it anyway.

Carlton's personality was different and the media made him seem weird. He got involved with Gus Hoefling with all that martial arts stuff, burying his arm in a tub of rice, that sort of thing. When Carlton was at his peak, it didn't pay, publicity-wise, to be different. He zipped his lips with the press and didn't do any of the television shows. He was always friendly to me. I guess he figured I couldn't misquote him or do him any harm.

I guess each case is different, but it always puzzled me why some big leaguers refused to talk to the media. It's just part of the job. The media represents the fans, the fans want to know more about the ballplayer, and management wants to sell tickets to fans.

Living in Philadelphia, I get involved in arguments all the time about Mike Schmidt. Was he the best third baseman to ever play the game?

Me, I still believe that Brooks Robinson was the best fielding third baseman I ever saw. If you want to add power, okay, then Schmidt was better overall. I'm not knocking Schmidt's fielding. He charged the ball, barehanded it, as well as anybody. He was another strange guy, who seemed too cool, too aloof, to satisfy Philadelphia's hard-to-please fans.

I guess I have my own crooked yardstick for measuring players.

Everyone tells me that Wayne Gretzky is the greatest hockey player who ever lived. I met him, shared a dais with him at the Victor awards. He loves baseball. And when I played Edmonton, he'd come out to the game. But my pick is Bobby Orr, the tough little guy who played for Boston. I know he was a defenseman, but he was a defenseman who could take the puck the length of the ice and score. I loved watching him.

My favorite football player was Steve Van Buren, the running back for the Eagles. Tough guy, who would have made it today, even with those 300-pound defensive linemen. I was a Chuck Bednarik fan too. There's a guy who played 60 minutes, offense and defense. I doubt if anybody could do that today. Among the quarterbacks, I really liked Sonny Jurgensen, as much because he was a free spirit as for his throwing ability.

I can't go along with the people who say Wilt Chamberlain was the greatest basketball player to ever play the game. When he broke in, who was there to give him a bad time? George Mikan? When Bill Russell came along, he represented a challenge. And Russell's teams won a lot more championships than Chamberlain's teams.

And there are some terrific centers around today. Houston's Hakeem Olajuwon is really good. And the guy with the Knicks, Patrick Ewing, can play. The big kid in Orlando, Shaquille O'Neal, tears down backboards. And now, the Sixers have a skinny seven-six guy named Shawn Bradley they're praying will lead them out of the doldrums.

In basketball, at least, I don't catch hell, because I agree that Michael Jordan is the best I've ever seen, someone who can do everything, and then, just when you think you've seen it all, he comes up with something different. I wouldn't want to be in his shoes, though. He lives in a fish bowl. And because of that, it was foolish for him to go to Atlantic City to gamble the night before a playoff game against the Knicks.

Does that mean he has a gambling problem? I'm not a psychiatrist. All I see is the stuff coming out about losing a million bucks on the golf course. I don't like the theory that a million bucks to him is like $10,000 to you and me. A million bucks, even if he makes $27,000,000 on those endorsements, is still a huge chunk of cash.

Plus, a gambling addicition puts those endorsements at risk.

Money seems to have lost its meaning for the superstars. Fine a guy like Charles Barkley $10,000 and he laughs at you. Barkley makes a commercial to sell sneakers and he says he doesn't want to be a role model. He's telling kids to buy his sneakers and don't copy the rest of him. Some message.

What's happened is that superstars seldom go back into the community they came from. They get paid for every appearance, so they see no reason to do freebies.

Growing up, my favorite fighter was Max Baer. Why not, he was half-Jewish, I liked that. He lost to Jimmy Braddock and my heart was broken. At AIEA Barracks I got to meet Freddy Apostoli, a terrific middleweight. I sold him a pair of my Navy pants for $10. Georgie Abrams was another fighter I liked. He never won a championship. Wound up parking cars at the Fontainbleu Hotel in Miami Beach after the war.

I got to meet Billy Conn at Toots Shor's one night. I was sitting there, being interviewed by Red Smith, when Conn came in. He should have won that fight with Joe Louis. Louis said, "He can run, but he can't hide." And Conn took the bait. He had the fight won, but no, he felt he had to slug with Louis, try and knock him out. I think it was Conn, or maybe Jerry Quarry, who said, "What's the good of being Irish, if you can't be stubborn?"

Louis was great, but my memory of him is spoiled by the "bum of the month" times, when he fought guys who had no chance. He beat up poor Tommy Farr, and the next day Farr came into the Steel Pier in Atlantic City, his eyes swollen, partly hidden behind dark glasses. I was about 14, out front, handing out programs. I had this silly hat on that didn't fit me, so I stuffed four rolls of paper in it, to hold it on. I'm out there clowning, dipsy-doodling while I'm handing out the programs. They finally fired me.

I was in Puerto Rico once, with Rocky Marciano, who retired undefeated (which sets him apart). I've seen those stories that talk about how cheap he was, but that's not so unusual. (A guy like Tommy Lasorda still has his recess money. Some guys, the check comes, they develop an impediment in their reach.) One of the most memorable fights I ever saw was Marciano against Joe Walcott. Murray Goodman was doing the publicity for the fight and he got me a ticket. Walcott had the fight won. He had busted up Rocky's face early. And now, he had him against the ropes, but he went to throw a right hand and Marciano nailed him. Boom!

I spent time with Jack Sharkey, when we did a sports

show together. (Sports shows were a big thing in those days.) He was a champion fly-caster.

Philadelphia has had its share of colorful guys. Joey Giardello is one of them, came through the ranks as a club fighter, had to wait forever to get a title shot. He was a brawler. He never heard of finesse. He'd walk in, take three to land two. And you didn't want to be in the same hotel room when he lost his temper. Man busted up more furniture than termites.

I got to know Dan Bucceroni, the heavyweight, real well. There's a guy who could throw a punch, but he had so much glass in his jaw he tinkled when he walked. Don Battles, another good friend, managed him. Dan was set for a title fight and decided to take a match with Tommy "Hurricane" Jackson while waiting. Bingo, Jackson jabbed Bucceroni all night. There was a guy who couldn't punch his way out of a paper bag, and he won the fight.

Maybe I'm with the majority when I pick Sugar Ray Robinson as the best fighter, pound for pound, I've ever seen.

I've seen them come and go, stars in every sport. And I've read about them all in the newspapers, and through the years, I've gotten to know a lot of sportswriters.

If you want to combine talent and character, Jim Murray ranks right up there at the top of the list for me. Maybe because he reminds me of myself. He's had more than his share of sadness in his life, yet he writes funny. Murray writes his column for the *Los Angeles Times*. Another guy who was kind to me preceded Murray at the *Times*—a guy named Vincent X. Flaherty.

Shirley Povich is another guy who ranks high on that combination of good writer, good human being. His son, Maury, has his own talk show now.

I surprise people when I tell them I really liked Dick Young of the *New York Daily News*. Young was a purist, a tough, no-nonsense writer. But somehow, he liked me, and we barnstormed together, raised money to fight multiple sclerosis.

Young didn't like Howard Cosell, and I didn't either. There's a guy who jumped to the top and forgot all the people he'd met along the way. There's a guy who became arrogant and thought he was more important than the sport he was covering.

When I performed with the Browns, I won over the two top columnists in St. Louis, Bob Broeg and Bob Burnes.

My favorite Chicago writer is Jerome Holtzman. Once you get past the cigar smoke, you find a guy with a big heart. He wrote one of the best baseball books ever written, *No Cheering in the Press Box*.

In Philadelphia, I always liked Ray Kelly, who covered baseball for the *Bulletin*. He loved to play golf, loved to bet horses. A few scotches, followed by a good steak, followed by baseball talk, and he was a happy man.

Most people think that Gene Mauch invented the double switch, where you bring a guy out of the bullpen and put him in the third slot in the batting order, so that, if that guy made the last out the previous inning, and you put the new rightfielder in the ninth spot, you maybe get an extra inning out of your relief pitcher. It was Ray Kelly who talked to Mauch about that, convinced him it was a smart way to use your bench strength.

Frank Dolson is another one of my favorite Philadelphia writers. Frank loves the game. Uses his vacation to go to minor league ballparks, to see the Philadelphia farm hands on their way up.

It's funny how some broadcasters get inflated reputations, and some get overlooked. I happen to think that Philadelphia fans are lucky to have Harry Kalas, Richie Ashburn, and Chris Wheeler doing the broadcasts of the Phillies games. There's a chemistry there that's special. Kalas gets his share of national attention when he does Notre Dame games, but Ashburn is content to just do the Phillies in his low-key style. (Ashburn is another guy who probably deserves to be in the Hall of Fame. There's a guy who hit .306 in his final season. But he's not bitter about being left out.)

One guy who deserves the praise is Ernie Harwell in

Detroit. I could never understand why they fired him, because he was an institution there. The year they let him go, I was in Oakland and he saw me in the lobby. He told me to wait, he went to his room, got his tape recorder, and taped an interview with me for his pre-game show.

One of the first guys to give me a boost was Jack Brickhouse in Chicago. He was televising a game where I was performing and he told the cameraman to stick with me, and that he would call the pitches like a guy doing radio.

Harry Caray is another guy who has been kind to me down through the years. Sometimes he could be tough on the ballplayers. They'd come off a road trip and their wives would tell them what Harry had said about them. He's got a great gimmick, singing "Take Me Out to the Ballgame" in the seventh inning, and he's made enough money that he can be honest when he's unhappy with what he sees on the field.

He's also opened a terrific restaurant in Chicago. Great veal chop.

It's scarey sometimes, appearing with sons of players I've known. And jolting to hear Skip Caray doing games out of Atlanta. When Skip's son, or Todd Kalas's son, start doing big league games, I'll know it's time to quit.

Chapter 20

KING FOR A DAY

I have to be the homeliest king since Henry VIII, but I felt positively, absolutely handsome the day I was crowned "King of Baseball."

It happened in Atlanta, at the Marriott Marquis Hotel, as part of the annual minor league meetings in early December, 1988. I'd gone to those meetings for about 18 straight years, sat through the annual dinner, applauded with a touch of envy every time they dimmed the lights and began reading the description of the man they had chosen as "King of Baseball" for that year.

After a while, I figured, what the hell, if they couldn't take a joke, that's their problem.

I didn't go to the annual meetings to hunt for bookings. I just went to be part of the scene, to see old friends. Some of the other acts had booths in the convention center area, people like Morganna, the Chicken, the Diamond Belles, the Dynamite Lady. And the manufacturers of novelty items had booths, too. They'd display the souvenir stuff they were making, and general managers would order stuff for give-away days the next season.

The directors of the National Association of Minor Leagues picks the person for "King of Baseball" and they keep it a secret.

I'm sitting there and as soon as they started reading the background, I knew it was me. How many guys have been out there for six decades, clowning? They introduce me, I walk up there, make a speech; they stick a crown on my head, a cape over my shoulders, give me a bat engraved with the details. (I gave the bat to my daughter to keep.) There were also two round-trip tickets anywhere American Airlines flew.

The speech was the one I gave in *Bull Durham*, the one about having my ashes spread at home plate. By the way, that's not the strangest last request I've come accross by any means.

There was a record promotions guy in Philadelphia named Matty Singer. Matty, the Humdinger, Singer. He promoted Jim Croce, the Villanova guy who got killed in a plane crash just when he was going to the top of the charts. When Matty died, I went to his funeral. The rabbi said he was reluctantly playing a tape that Matty had left behind. He turns it on, you hear Matty saying that he didn't want anybody to mourn for him. He said he wanted air conditioning, a tape recorder in his coffin filled with the biggest hits he had promoted, and he wanted to be buried face down. That way, everybody could slowly walk past his coffin and kiss his ass.

I used to kid around and say that when I died, I wanted to be buried near first base, with my nose sticking in the air. That way, when guys ran around first, if they tripped over my nose, they'd say, "Max Patkin, you son-of-a-gun, you're still getting in the way."

Tommy Lasorda used to talk about "The Big Dodger in the Sky" and how, when he died, he wanted the Dodgers schedule on his tombstone, that way, if anyone came to visit his grave they'd know if there was a ballgame in town that night.

Anyway, the people who were happiest about me being named King of Baseball were the scouts, the guys who have sat through my act time after time. I know guys like Tom Ferrick were rooting for me. I got to know him while I was in the Navy. I pitched against him. He played on a team with Johnny Mize, Hugh Casey, and some other big leaguers.

Tom was a pretty good hitting pitcher who pitched with the Yankees and the Senators later on. This ballgame, we had rallied to tie the score in the ninth. Now, 10th inning, Tom was the first hitter. Vinnie Smith was my catcher. He caught in the big leagues for a while, and then became an umpire. He knew I had a good fastball, and a mediocre curve. But, for some reason, he called for a curve. I threw it, I hung it, Ferrick hit it out of the ballpark. First hitter, first pitch, bam, the game was over. He still kids me about that pitch.

Being crowned King of Baseball was a big honor and I enjoyed the moment (my *biggest* thrill in baseball is still that first day with Cleveland, with 80,000 in the stands). The Smithsonian Institute in Washington also honored me one year. Me, Bob Feller, and Enos Slaughter. They invited us to Washington for something they called "Baseball Day." They set us up behind tables, and we talked about what we had done in baseball.

I remember having dinner with Slaughter the night before. We were talking about the Hall of Fame and he said, "I've told my daughters that if I'm not elected to the Hall of Fame when I'm alive [and eventually he was], and they want to put me in after I die, I want them to tell the committee to stick the Hall of Fame plaque where the sun never shines."

I thought he belonged. And I think Phil Rizzuto belongs. His numbers are similar to Pee wee Reese's numbers, and Pee wee has been in for a while. Nobody bunted better than Rizzuto. And he held that Yankee infield together. I get a kick out of listening to him broadcast games, calling people "huckleberry," and leaving early to beat the traffic.

One of the nicest things that ever happened to me was being named Man of the Year by the Jewish Basketball League Alumni in Philadelphia. They were ahead of their time, because one year they switched to Woman of the Year and honored Sally Rand, the legendary stripteaser. She stood up and said, "This is the first time I ever got applause with my clothes on."

In 1979, they honored me, but it was bittersweet. Eddie Gottlieb, who had never missed the banquet in 41 years, was in Temple Hospital after major surgery. Bill Veeck sent a telegram that they read that said, "Congratulations to without a doubt the ugliest, the funniest, and the finest entertainer in baseball history—

and incidentally to a very dear friend."

I'm in the West Philadelphia High School Hall of Fame. I haven't been back to see where they've got my picture. That's a tough place to visit these days, but so are most inner city schools. I'm in the Philadelphia Hall of Fame, and, again, I'm not sure where they've got my picture. And around 1985 I was inducted into the Pennsylvania Sports Hall of Fame, along with Elmer Valo, Roger Penske, and Tom Ferrick. That was a nice honor.

One of the nicest gifts I ever received was a photo from the son of Emmit Kelly, the circus clown who worked for the Dodgers for a while. He said that his father and I were the two best clowns in the world. That made me feel good.

Not many people know there's a Clown Hall of Fame. It's in Delavan, Wisconsin. I was inducted in 1991 when I got the Clown Hall of Fame Lifetime of Laughter Achievement Award. It goes to people who have contributed to letting the laughter loose, to those who have helped make this world a happier place. The year I was honored, Bobby Kaye, Frankie Saluto, Glenn Little, Michael Polakov, Dan Rice and Aye Jaye were honored too.

I'm better known in other cities than I am in my hometown, and that's understandable. I've been clowning for 50 years and I can count the number of Philadelphia appearances on my fingers. Well, maybe my fingers and my toes.

My dream of pitching for the Phillies died early. There was that tryout, back around 1937. Hans Lobert was the manager, I remember that. And the Phillies still played in Baker Bowl. They'd bring prospects in and let them pitch batting practice. They don't do that now. They have radar guns and they let the kid pitch on the side, or in the bullpen. That way, they don't risk someone getting hit in the head by some wild-eyed teenager.

My tryout was brief, because that's the day Chuck Klein hammered a line drive back at me, that hit my foot. I didn't get that foot back inside the door until Bill Veeck hired me to coach and clown with the Indians, and Cleveland came to Philadelphia to play the A's.

I scrounged around, begged and borrowed extra passes from players who weren't using them. I guess I left 20 free passes for family and friends.

Bob Feller started that day for Cleveland. He was pitching one of his greatest games ever, against the A's. He struck out 11 of the first 13—something awesome like that. And then, his spikes caught, and he fell off the mound and hurt his knee. He had to leave the game.

I also remember that Ferris Fain was back in the lineup after a long time on the disabled list. Fain had a vicious temper, and one day he kicked the first base bag and broke his ankle.

He'd been out five or six weeks and now he was back in the lineup. I knew Fain because we'd been in the service together. I go out to coach at first base and I turn to the crowd and I yell, "Imitation of Ferris Fain!" I kick the bag, fall down, grab my ankle, thrash around like I'm in pain. The crowd loved it.

I came to Philadelphia in 1951, when I was with the Browns. I took more people to dinner than they had in the stands in those days.

Once I performed at an exhibition game, the Phillies against a sandlot team that played at 69th and Dicks Avenue. Would I make that up? I can't recall how that came about. Some politician must have arranged it. This was strictly a sandlot field, no ticket booths, no turnstiles. They didn't charge admission. Maybe they passed the hat.

It had to be around '48 or '49. Maje McDonald, my old teammate from Brown Prep, was a coach with the Phillies then. We were regarded as the Mutt and Jeff of baseball when we teamed up. He's a little, spunky guy and he had a good career at Villanova, where he captained the basketball team.

As a pitcher, he had a good curve, but he never had a major league fast ball. He wound up coaching with the Phillies, got some unfair publicity in recent years when people looked back on Jackie Robinson's first visit to Philadelphia and accused Maje of shouting racist stuff at Robinson from the dugout. I don't think Maje has a bad bone in his body, and all the time I was around him, I never saw any signs of prejudice. Maje denied it happened, and I believe him.

I did have one chance to perform with the Phillies, but that got squelched by the owner. Bill Giles was the promotions director in those days and he wanted me to perform at the Junior Baseball Federation charity exhibition between the Phillies and the Orioles. Bob Carpenter, who owned the club, said he didn't want a clown out there, making a farce of the game.

That year, they had coaches pitching, infielders playing the outfield, callups from the minor leagues pitching for both sides. By the sixth inning, it was a joke. I would have fit in perfectly in a game like that, but no dice.

I guess the best testimonials are the repeat bookings. Craig Stein, the guy who owns the Reading franchise, told writers I was "a piece of Americana, a Norman Rockwell painting come to life."

The first year he bought the club, he leased it back to Joe Buzas, an old friend. Joe had a fierce temper, and I put it to the test that season. He was sitting in a box seat when I came out to do my act. I strutted over there like I was going to shake his hand and I slapped a big gooey pie in his face. Buzas is moving the Portland team to Salt Lake City, to a brand-new stadium with 12,000 seats and 24 sky boxes. I'm looking forward to performing there for a guy I've known for 37 years.

He told writers that I was a part of the lore of minor-league baseball. And how people, young and old, enjoy my routines. He says he won't ever forget that night when he was sitting in his dugout and I reached into the bag of game balls and started tossing them into the stands. He started screaming and I kept tossing and the fans loved it.

Ed Holtz, who's the general manager in Macon, is another guy who has stuck with me down through the years. He says he knows my routine as well as I do, and the thing he likes best about me is that I perform the same whether there's a full house or empty stands.

When there's a small crowd, he loves the line I use: "I had more people in my bed last night than there are here... what a bleeping town."

Miles Wolff, president of Baseball America, is another guy who likes my act. He called me "a national treasure." And he once said, "Max Patkin can bring a smile to anyone, but how does he hold all that water in his mouth?"

Chapter 21

THE ENDLESS SUMMER

I don't collect matchbook covers, menus or memorabilia.

I don't paint. I don't do needlepoint. (Don't laugh. Rosey Grier, the huge tackle who used to play for the Los Angeles Rams, does needlepoint.)

I don't have any hobbies—unless you count gin rummy.

I don't belong to the Book of the Month Club.

I don't gamble on ballgames, I don't drink, I don't smoke, I don't chase women. (I amble after women, but I don't chase. I'm like the dog that chases cars down the street. What's he gonna do if he catches one? He can't drive!)

I'm not one of those people who buries his head in a book the moment the stewardess says "Buckle your seatbelt."

All of which makes for some long days and some longer nights on the road.

Most minor league ballgames start at 7:30. The umpires hustle the players along, none of that step out, tug on the batting glove, grab your crotch, knock dirt out of your spikes ritual some big league hitters go through after every pitch.

I do my act in the third, fourth, fifth innings, and I'm done. But I need time to cool down, to shower, to get the filthy uniform washed by the clubhouse guy, and to comb what's left of my hair.

I stick around after that, sit with the scouts, pick up my paycheck, and head back to the motel. If it's a big city, the dining room is still open and I can grab a sandwich. Otherwise, I'm at the mercy of the fast food joints that are open that late.

And then it's back to the room and loneliness until the alarm goes off and it's time to move on to the next town.

If I read books or kept a diary or whittled, I'd have something to do to kill those lonely hours. Instead, I depend on television. Which makes me an expert on late night TV. Which means I miss Johnny Carson. He was funny, but more important, he seemed to listen to his guests. He didn't mind setting them up with straight lines.

Ed McMahon, a guy from Philadelphia, was the perfect foil for him. He laughed loud and took the drinking jokes and the divorce jokes good naturedly, and he could bail Carson out of a jam when a joke flopped.

What I liked best was the skits, the Mighty Carson Art Players. And the bit with Karnac the Magnificent, where he'd wear the turban and give the answer and then rip open the envelope and read the question.

That's dumb, but cute. Like my act.

I don't think Jay Leno is funny enough. I don't think he gets enough out of his guests. I don't like David Letterman because he's snotty. He doesn't give his guests any room to be funny. He embarrasses them. And he's got that fake laugh that bothers me. And I'm not too crazy about Arsenio Hall either. He laughs at everything, makes all those whoo-whoo noises, sits there clutching himself like a kid.

Mornings, I like Phil Donahue best. Asks tough questions, listens to the answers. I don't stay tuned when he's got transvestite cab drivers or women who fool around with their husband's brothers.

I guess my favorite show on television is "L.A. Law." The actors are terrific, the stories seem real, especially the courtroom scenes. I like "20/20" too. And "60 Minutes," although I tell people that my brother Eddie is so slow, it takes him 90 minutes to watch "60 Minutes."

I've been on the road so long, I can remember when Jackie Gleason first started "The Honeymooners." I loved that show. Everybody could identify with that guy. The thing is, I knew Gleason before he made it big on television. He used to work in some dives in Philadelphia as a standup comic.

That's one thing I could never be, a standup comic. The nightclub life would depress me. A tough audience, smoking, drinking, trying to impress their dates. Late hours, tough to unwind when you've finished your act. I've seen too many guys turn to drink or drugs to keep them going.

I've been on the road so long I can remember when you got your exercise getting up to change the channels. No remote clickers then. And the sets were black and white. A guy named "Madman Muntz" was the "Crazy Eddie" of his day and Milton Berle was king of television comedy. He had "The Texaco Star Theatre."

When I was a kid I used to read fairy tales. And then, I switched to biographies. Now, I seldom read a book. I guess the last one I really liked was *Veeck as in Wreck*, even though he described me as a guy with a touch of the gutter in him.

"If he wasn't getting the laughter he expected," Veeck wrote, "his contortions would begin to border on the obscene. The first season we had him with us, I'd always watch him like a hawk. As soon as he began to drift toward bad taste, I'd bellow out, 'Nooooooo, Max, nooooooo!'"

I don't remember it that way, but I will admit that my language gets a little earthy sometimes. My brother squawks about that too, says I try to sound like the ballplayers, and he's probably right.

I read the *Philadelphia Daily News* and the *Philadelphia Inquirer* every day, front to back. I'll read *USA Today* two or three times a week. I'll read *Baseball America, The Sporting News*, even though it's gone downhill. They've let go most of the outstanding writers they used to have.

I can't read a book on an airplane because my eyes get tired. It's strange, but I had to get nailed by line drives as a young pitcher before I'd agree to get my eyes tested. They found out I needed glasses. Later on, I got contacts.

In my younger days I loved the movies. Mostly westerns. I loved *High Noon* and *Red River,* and I can remember John Wayne in *Stagecoach.*

When it came to actresses, I liked the ones with big boobs, somebody like Janet Leigh. As a kid, I stood outside the State Theatre to get Fifi D'Orsey's autograph. Honest, I was nine years old. I had seen her in *All Quiet on the Western Front* and she was terrific. The only woman in the movie, and she came to make an appearance at the State Theatre.

When I was in the Navy, I wrote to a lot of actresses and asked for autographed pictures. Which is why guys loved to hang around my bunk, because I had Lana Turner and Rita Hayworth pictures that were terrific.

One of these days I'm going to dig through the rubble in my closets and find those pictures.

Chapter 22

CASEY AT THE BAT

I got to know Casey Stengel when he managed the Yankees and he'd come to St. Louis to play the Browns. Bill Veeck would invite Casey to the Chase Hotel nightclub and we'd sit there and have a few laughs.

Casey had that funny way of walking, because he'd been hit by a taxi years ago. I think the Boston writers wanted to vote the cab driver the most valuable player award that year. Casey also had a funny way of talking, which endeared him to the New York writers, because they loved the idea of having a character manage the Yankees. When they held his final press conference, one of the New York writers yelled, "Associated Press says you've been fired." Stengel never batted an eye. He yelled back at the guy, "What does United Press say?"

When the New York guys had to deal with Yogi Berra, they made up clever things for him. I'm sure he said some of them, like the time somebody recommended a famous restaurant and Yogi said, "Nobody goes there any more—it's too crowded."

And when he was promoting the chocolate drink, Yoo-Hoo, and he came to Philadelphia, one of the sportswriters asked him if Yoo-Hoo was hyphenated, and Yogi said, "It ain't even carbonated."

Now, some of those New York guys are trying to make Ralph Kiner seem funny. I know one thing, Kiner isn't intentionally funny.

Thinking about Stengel and Berra makes me think about managers I've enjoyed being around through the years.

Mickey Vernon had to be one of my all-time favorites. Good guy, low-key, never forgot our Navy days. Tony

LaRussa, who managed the Oakland A's, gives me a hug every time he sees me. Lou Boudreau belongs in my top five, because he stuck by me in Cleveland, when the critics were ripping me.

I liked Jack McKeon, a guy I first met when he was managing in Vancouver. He was ahead of his time. He had a two-way radio hooked up with his pitcher. He could tell the guy what to throw without using signals from the dugout that the other team might steal. He only used it for a little while. Too much static.

Alvin Dark was another guy ahead of his time. He loved to match wits with Gene Mauch. Once he started one pitcher, had two other guys warming up in the bullpen and another guy in the clubhouse runway. Dark got in trouble when a *Newsday* sportswriter named Stan Isaacs quoted him about black players, but I never saw that side of him. To me, he seemed deeply religious. A lot of people don't realize that he was an outstanding football player before he turned to baseball. I saw him when he was the quarterback for a Marine team in Honolulu.

I sympathized with the tough time Frank Robinson had in Cleveland, how hard Gaylord Perry made it for him, squawking about his salary. I was booked in there for the last day of the season, and Ken Aspromonte knew he was going to get fired. I asked Aspromonte what I could do on the field, and he said, "Max, you can crap all over home plate, do anything you want, I don't give a damn."

Earl Weaver managed Robinson in those glory years in Baltimore. Lots of people thought Weaver was a grump, but he loved me, for some reason. He showed it the first time I met him. He was managing in Appleton, Wisconsin. We had a full house. And then the lights fail. All they had left were some dim lights over the infield. Weaver said they'd play three innings, so I could do my act, and get paid. He even played in the game himself.

I saw him again, years later, in Elmira. This time I was sitting behind home plate with Eddie Sawyer, who was scouting. Weaver went crazy over an umpire's call, ranted and raved and kicked dirt. Sawyer thought the guy was out of control, thought he'd wind up in an insane asylum.

When Weaver managed in Rochester, the owner didn't want me to go on for some reason. He was going to pay me not to perform. But Weaver told him I would tone down my act, and he even let me coach third. I sent a runner home, and he won the game, 1–0. Maybe that's why he liked me.

I've had good rapport with the commissioners down through the years. Happy Chandler helped me in the early days, but after that, it's not exactly a parade of memorable men.

Bowie Kuhn, who got fired by the owners, liked me. He brought his family to see me perform in Greenwood, South Carolina. The general manager there, Charlie Avranian, was sharp, and when Kuhn got the job as commissioner, he invited Kuhn to make his first official visit to a ballpark, the park in Greenwood.

It's tough being commissioner because the owners hire you and expect you to do what they want you to do. I don't think I'd want that job. Not enough laughs, not enough authority. Bill White found that out when he got tired of being National League president. He thought he could do some good, but then he found out his hands were tied.

Chapter 23

THE STREAK SHATTERS

What does a baseball clown do on his day off?

He goes to the ballpark if he's as dumb, and as stubborn, as Max Patkin.

Which explains why I slipped on the clubhouse steps at Fenway Park in Boston on a day off in August, 1993, severely sprained my left ankle, turning it a woeful blue, which is how the rest of me felt too.

Why Boston? Why Fenway Park? Why me?

I had done a streak of 16 games in 18 days, from Bend, Oregon, back to Wilmington, Delaware to South Dakota, criss-crossing the country. I had a date in Glen Falls, New York, followed by an open date, followed by an appearance in Binghamton, New York. I thought about using the open date to zip into New York because the Yankees were at home and I have a fondness for George Steinbrenner, who booked me into Yankee Stadium years ago.

The first gloomy omen came when I got rained out in Glen Falls. Only the second washout of the season for me.

I checked the schedule , I checked the maps. The Red Sox were at home the next day and New Brittain was only a two-hour bus ride from Boston. I'd have the chance to see my good friend, Johnny Pesky, the Red Sox were in the pennant race. Why not?

I've known Pesky since my Navy days. I pitched against his team and he got three infield singles off me in one game. If he didn't have those good legs he never would have made it to the big leagues. I called him "The Leg Man." Every winter I speak at his banquet in Lynn, Massachusetts. They honor him, year after year after year—every February—and they fill the hall to capacity every time.

I had phoned Lou Gorman, the general manager, and

he left me a field pass and a lunchroom pass. They had a jammed press box because of the pennant race and he said he'd put me in the ESPN booth, which sounded good. He said he'd put my name up on the scoreboard, let everybody know I was there. Gorman had booked me in Kinston, North Carolina, maybe 30 years ago.

I caught the commuter flight out of Albany, got to the Boston airport, Pesky picked me up in a limo. We went to his house first, said we had to play some gin rummy, for old time's sake. I told him, half-cent a point, single game— no Hollywood style, where you play three games at once.

I still managed to lose $3 to him. He laughed, said, "Max, you're still a stiff." He threw the four of diamonds at one point. Another four was dead in the discard heap. I'd already taken the three of diamonds from him. I needled him.

He said, "Max, I don't have to think when I play you."

Another bad omen.

We had lunch in Lynn, at his favorite joint, and then we went to the ballpark. He said he had to get dressed because he hits fungoes to the infielders. I stuck around the clubhouse, kibitzing with the coaches, with the players. And then, I started down the steps towards the field. I missed the bottom step somehow. I thought I'd broken something because I heard something snap and I fell clumsily.

I knew right away, laying there in a heap, that I was going to be out of action. I knew my consecutive game streak, over 4,000 games without missing one because of injury or illness, was over.

The left ankle started to swell right away. They helped me out to the dugout and I sat there on the bench, my leg propped up. Roger Clemens, their ace pitcher, came by. I'm sitting there, helpless, in pain, foot raised, and he walks past without a word. Same with Mo Vaughn, a player I knew from the minors, a guy I sat next to on the dais at a winter banquet. Nothing.

Finally, a radio guy came over, said he'd seen me in *Bull Durham*, wondered what happened. Then he interviewed me for about eight minutes. Ed Farmer, who once pitched for the Phillies, and is now a broadcaster for the White Sox, came by, looking concerned. He's a helluva guy. I told him what happened and he said he'd use it during the broadcast.

A Dr. Foley came to look at me, got me moved to the First Aid room. He examined me, said I had to go to Jewish Hospital for X-rays. They took me to the emergency room, a woman doctor said it was a severe sprain, nothing broken.

I told her what I do for a living and she said she strongly urged me not to do it for the next two to three weeks. She said I ought to get one of those lightweight air casts to support the ankle.

They gave me a set of crutches and I hobbled out of there and went back to the ballpark. I got to sit in the ESPN booth all right, but Danny Darwin was pitching a no-hitter and Chris Berman, the announcer, wasn't about to tell the world that Max Patkin's consecutive-game streak, over 50 years, had ended.

Pesky wanted to leave, to beat the traffic. We listened to the game on the car radio, and a guy finally got a base hit off Darwin, so I didn't feel too badly about leaving a no-hitter. I stayed at Pesky's house in Swampscot and the next day we went to a deli there, where a judge and some other leading citizens in the town meet all the time. They sat there, I told them some of my stories for about an hour, and then Pesky drove me to the airport. They had a wheelchair waiting for me, the whole bit.

And then came the toughest part, calling New Brittain, Binghamton, and Reading to cancel. It was a strange feeling.

Binghamton wanted me to come up there anyway, give away my baseball card, sign some autographs, throw out the first ball. I flew up there, hobbling around on crutches. The rain had left the field looking like a swamp. They delayed the game for an hour and 45 minutes and the umpires were ready to toss the general manager out of his ballpark.

They wanted to call the game, he had a big crowd, and

he said they could get the field playable. They finally did. They were playing a Canadian team, so after both anthems, they brought me out there. I wasn't going to limp out there on crutches, so I left them in the dugout. I couldn't put any weight on the left ankle, so I couldn't throw a strike. I got a good hand anyway, signed autographs, and got a nice fee just for showing up.

Reading, two nights later, anticipated a good crowd for a doubleheader. They were giving away pennants with my picture on them and they wanted me in uniform. I got there, they had close to 8,000 people, a huge crowd. They brought me out in a golf cart between games of the doubleheader.

I made a two- or three-minute speech, told them how I'd gotten hurt, told them they were the greatest audience I'd ever seen, told them how I'd performed in Reading for 34 of the last 35 years, and that even though I would probably retire the next year, I would come back and make one more appearance in Reading.

I got a standing ovation. And then I went to the picnic area down the rightfield line to sign autographs. If they wanted a signed baseball card it was a buck apiece and I signed 300 of those.

I signed everything put in front of me, and nobody had ever seen a line as long as the line that formed. All the way down the first base side of the ballpark, past home plate. I signed from the start of the second game, until 20 minutes after the game was over.

Lou Reda, my buddy, who lives in Easton, had bought 25 tickets to the game. Now, he shows up with seven kids for autographs. He wasn't about to wait in a line a block long, so he tells them he's my manager, and he hustles to the front of the line saying, "Max, here are the kids from the orphanage I told you about." I'm half-groggy, so I don't know whether he's telling the truth or not, so I sign for all seven kids and wish them luck.

One of the other kids in line, a little girl about 10 years old, told me how touched she was with the speech I'd made.

Stan Hochman wrote a small story about the accident,

the end of the streak, for the *Philadelphia Daily News*. And then the Associated Press picked it up and it went out all over the country.

They used the item in *USA Today*, and the Boston paper printed a picture of me. And I started to get phone calls from all over the country, people concerned about me, sad that the streak was over, glad that I didn't break something else.

I've thought about retiring for a long time. Besides the loneliness of the road, there's the physical side of it, the creaky knees that keep me from doing some of the things I used to do.

I thought, if the bookings ever slacked off—under 25 a year let's say—I'd know it was time to hang 'em up.

But that's never happened.

So, then I thought, when the laughter dies, that's when I'll know it's time.

But that hasn't happened.

I worked with Ken Griffey, I worked with Ken Griffey Jr. I worked with Bobby and Barry Bonds. That's understandable, sons of famous fathers. But years ago, I roomed with Ray Boone. And I worked with his son, Bob Boone (one of the most durable catchers in big league history). And now I've worked with Bret Boone, Bob's kid, Ray's grandson.

Three generations, it makes you stop and think.

I come off a long road trip, maybe eight games in 10 days, and I have to bring the uniform to Jim Napoleon, the custom tailor who has stitched the thing together for the last 30 years.

The uniform is stitched together. I'm stitched together. It's a corny act, but it works. Why fix it? Why scrap it?

More and more lately, I think about what Nick Altrock told me the first time he saw me. He worked with Al Schacht all those years, even though they didn't get along.

He watched me perform and he called me over, and he said, "Kid, I loved your act. You quit when you were ahead."

I think about that a lot these days.

A MESSAGE FROM THE PUBLISHER

I was 12 years old when I first saw Max Patkin. It was at the old Texas Oilers ballpark in Tulsa, Oklahoma, and I had gotten in free in the fifth inning when they quit taking tickets. The next time I saw Max was at a hotel in Washington, D.C., where we met to discuss this book. He was 73 years old, and, I swear, just as fluid and funny as I remembered him as a boy. Max has seen firsthand more baseball than any person this century; it's a kid's dream come true to be able to publish his book.

W. R. Spence, M.D.
Publisher

At WRS Publishing, we are only interested in producing books we can be proud of—books that focus on people and/or issues that enlighten and inspire, books that change lives for the better, either through the celebration of human achievement or the revelation of human folly. **Call us at 1-800-299-3366 for suggestions or for a free book catalog.**

WATCH FOR THESE RELATED TITLES:

LIFE ON THE LINE, the moving story of all-pro lineman Karl Nelson, who came through the cancer that ended his football career with the New York Giants.

YOUNG AT HEART outlines the running career of 85-year-old Johnny Kelley—who has answered the starting gun at 63 Boston Marathons—and of long distance running in America in this Century.

PUSHING THE LIMITS, the story of John Howard, the "incredible human machine"—Olympic cyclist, world champion triathlete, holder of the world speed record (152 MPH on a bicycle)... and the list goes on.

DECEMBER CHAMPIONS, the account of 25 people aged over 75, who are still active in a wide variety of athletic endeavors.

WRS
PUBLISHING

A Division of WRS Group, Inc.
Waco, Texas